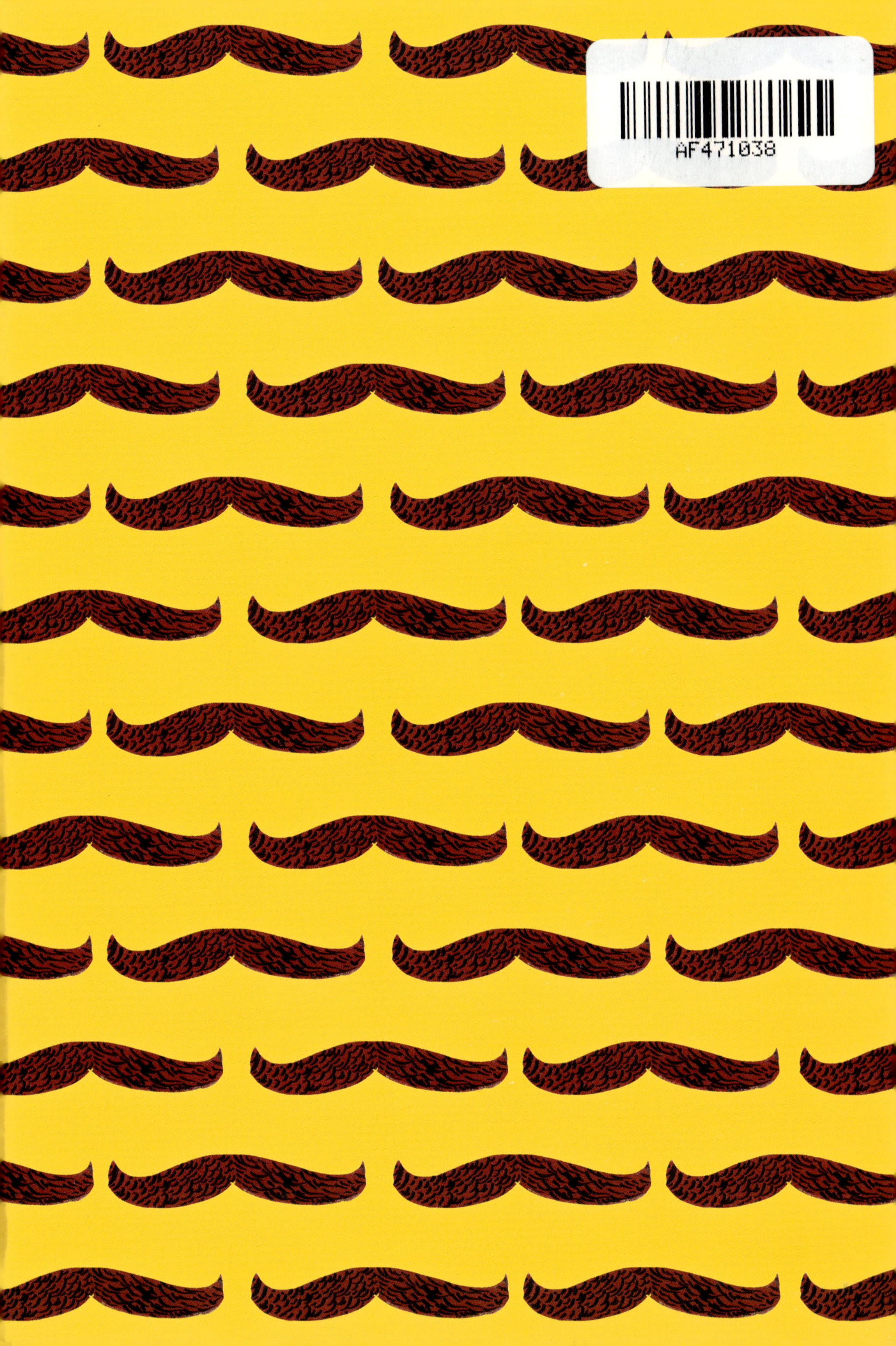
AF471038

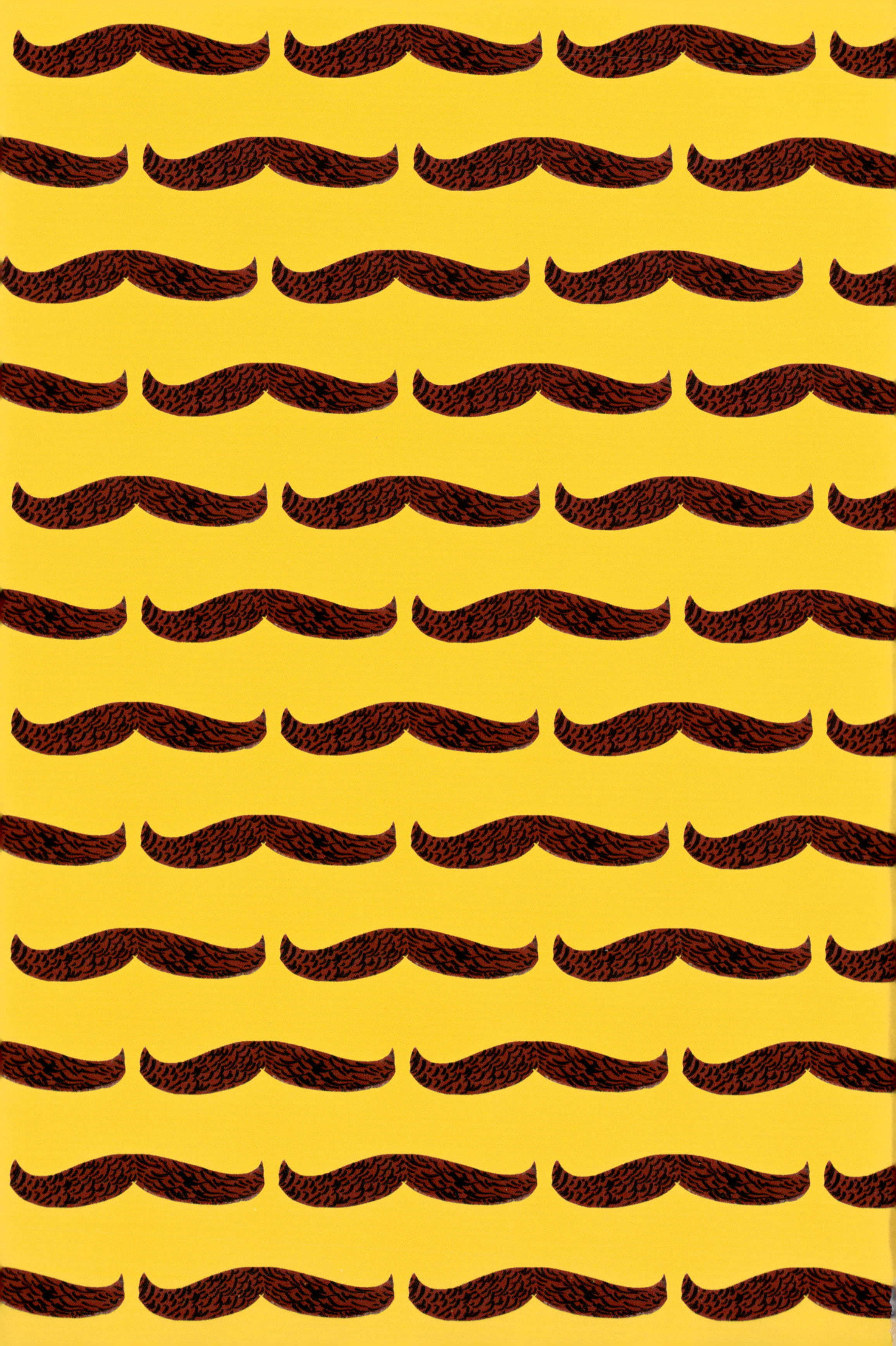

Published to accompany the project
Central line series
Central line
2011–2013

Curated by Charlotte Bonham-Carter, Louise Coysh,
Tamsin Dillon, Cathy Haynes and Snejana Krasteva.
Commissioned and produced by Art on the Underground,
with generous support from The National Lottery through
Arts Council England.

Edited by Charlotte Bonham-Carter, Louise Coysh,
Tamsin Dillon and Snejana Krasteva.
Copy edited by Melissa Larner.
Designed by Rose.
Endpapers: Bob and Roberta Smith and Tim Newton,
from *Who is Community?*, 2012.

Black Dog Publishing Limited
10A Acton Street
London
WC1X 9NG
United Kingdom
Tel: +44 (0)20 7713 5097
Fax: +44 (0)20 7713 8682
info@blackdogonline.com
www.blackdogonline.com

British Library Cataloguing-in-Publication Data.

A CIP record for this book is available from the British Library.
ISBN: 978 1 907317 90 3

Black Dog Publishing Limited, London, UK, is an environmentally responsible
company. This publication is printed on sustainably sourced paper.

Image Credits
pp. 10–11: courtesy of Capital Transport
pp. 13, 83: copyright TfL from the
London Transport Museum collection
pp. 22–23, 42–43, 49, 50–51, 52: Daisy Hutchison
pp. 28–29, 42–43, 44–45, 46–47, 75, 76–77, 78–79, 85:
Benedict Johnson
pp. 34–35, 60, 67, 68–69, 72–73, 87: Thierry Bal
p. 40, 46–47: courtesy of Michael Landy
p. 45: copyright London Evening Standard
(originally published 2/9/2011 by Kirsty Whalley)
p. 54: Ruth Ewan, copyright Laburnum Boat Club
pp. 55, 56– 57: Ruth Ewan
p. 57: courtesy of David Leboff
p. 71: courtesy of The Approach
p. 85: Alastair Fyfe

MAYOR OF LONDON

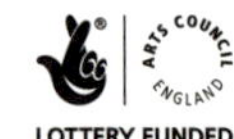

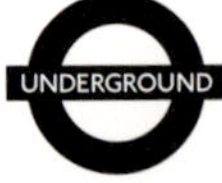

Transport for London

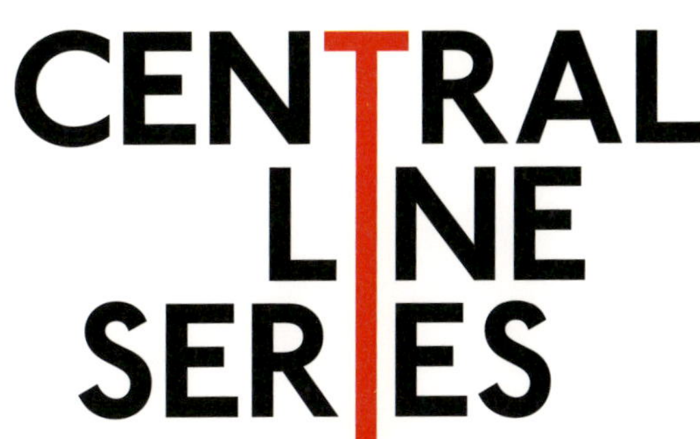
CENTRAL
LINE
SERIES

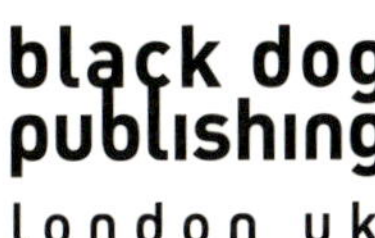
black dog
publishing
london uk

Contents

Foreword

The journey across London from White City, Ealing or West Ruislip in the west, through the centre of the city to Stratford, Leytonstone or Epping in the east, can be made in many ways: by bus, foot, bike and car—even by boat. The challenge is not the length of the trip, but that it involves passing through the largest urban metropolis in Europe. The most efficient way to take the journey is undoubtedly to use London Underground's Central line. The longest line on the Tube network, it passes through 12 London boroughs and interconnects with all other Tube lines.

That historic line is the focus of the third in an on-going series of line-based art projects by Art on the Underground: The Central line series. This publication brings together images of the work produced, including new artworks devised for and presented in trains and stations, along with specially commissioned essays and re-published texts that broaden the context for, and offer further perspectives on, the project.

The challenges associated with delivering a good Tube service are particularly acute on the Central line, and communication lies at the heart of dealing with the many demanding situations that arise on a daily basis. The relationship and communication between east and west, whether in regard to the Tube, to London, or to an international context, is an evocative subject. The Central line series project draws this local/global parallel to explore communication and exchange between individuals and groups of people in a range of situations. Communities, the languages used within and between them, and new technologies that are reshaping society and social interactions, are key factors for the project. Taking inspiration from the diversity of people and places spanned by the line, and the connections, relationships and situations that develop through them, the artworks also operate in a worldwide context. In addition to the new artworks, a discursive programme of events, talks and discussions and filmed interviews for podcasts has been a vital and critical element of the Central line series.

This book provides a crucial opportunity to acknowledge and thank, on behalf of Transport for London, all those involved in the project. The enormous task of bringing the commissions to fruition alongside the discursive programme and the development of this publication has been delivered by a tremendously dedicated Art on the Underground team, each member of which deserves gratitude and congratulations.

Thanks also to the many other organisations and individuals who have worked with us, in keeping with the idea of collaboration at the heart of this series, and have made vital contributions to ensure the successful delivery of sometimes complex projects.

In particular, we thank Create Festival, Chisenhale Gallery, Whitechapel Gallery, Barbican Art Gallery, the Laburnum Boat Club, the Museum of Childhood, and all the Stratford Rising organisations—including Stratford Circus, Stratford East Picture House, University of East London, Theatre Royal Stratford East, Rosetta Art Centre and The Nunnery.

We are hugely grateful for the support of the Arts Council of England through the lottery grant for the arts, without whose help these projects could not be presented to the audience of millions who use the Tube.

Ultimately, the biggest acknowledgement must go to the artists who worked to produce the excellent new works that are now collectively known as The Central line series. I would like to thank them for taking up these opportunities and for the enduring passion that they continue to show in their remarkable artistic practices. It is a privilege to work with them and to be able add these new works to the growing and powerful canon of art commissioned and presented by Art on the Underground.

Tamsin Dillon, Head of Art on the Underground

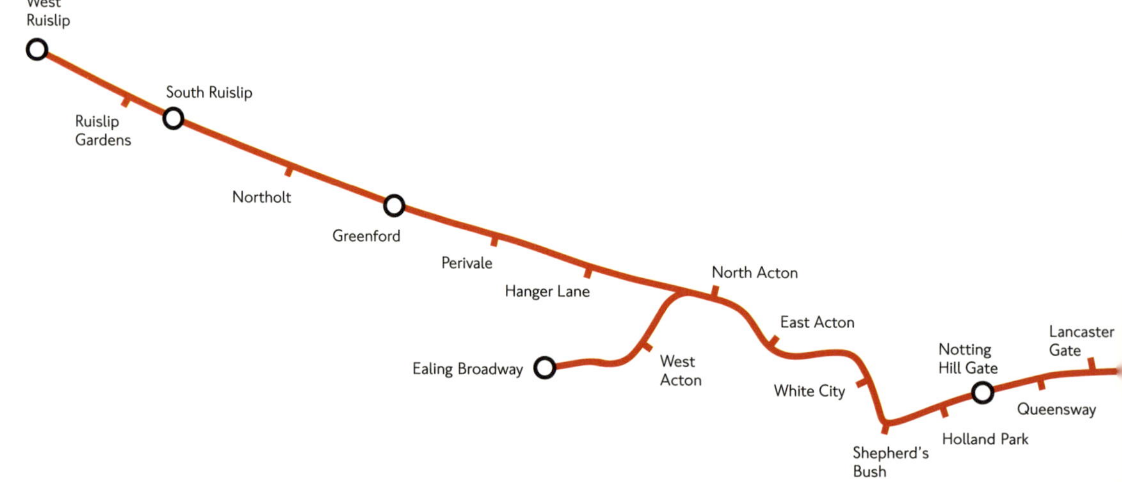

West Ruislip
South Ruislip
Ruislip Gardens
Northolt
Greenford
Perivale
Hanger Lane
North Acton
East Acton
Ealing Broadway
West Acton
White City
Shepherd's Bush
Notting Hill Gate
Holland Park
Queensway
Lancaster Gate

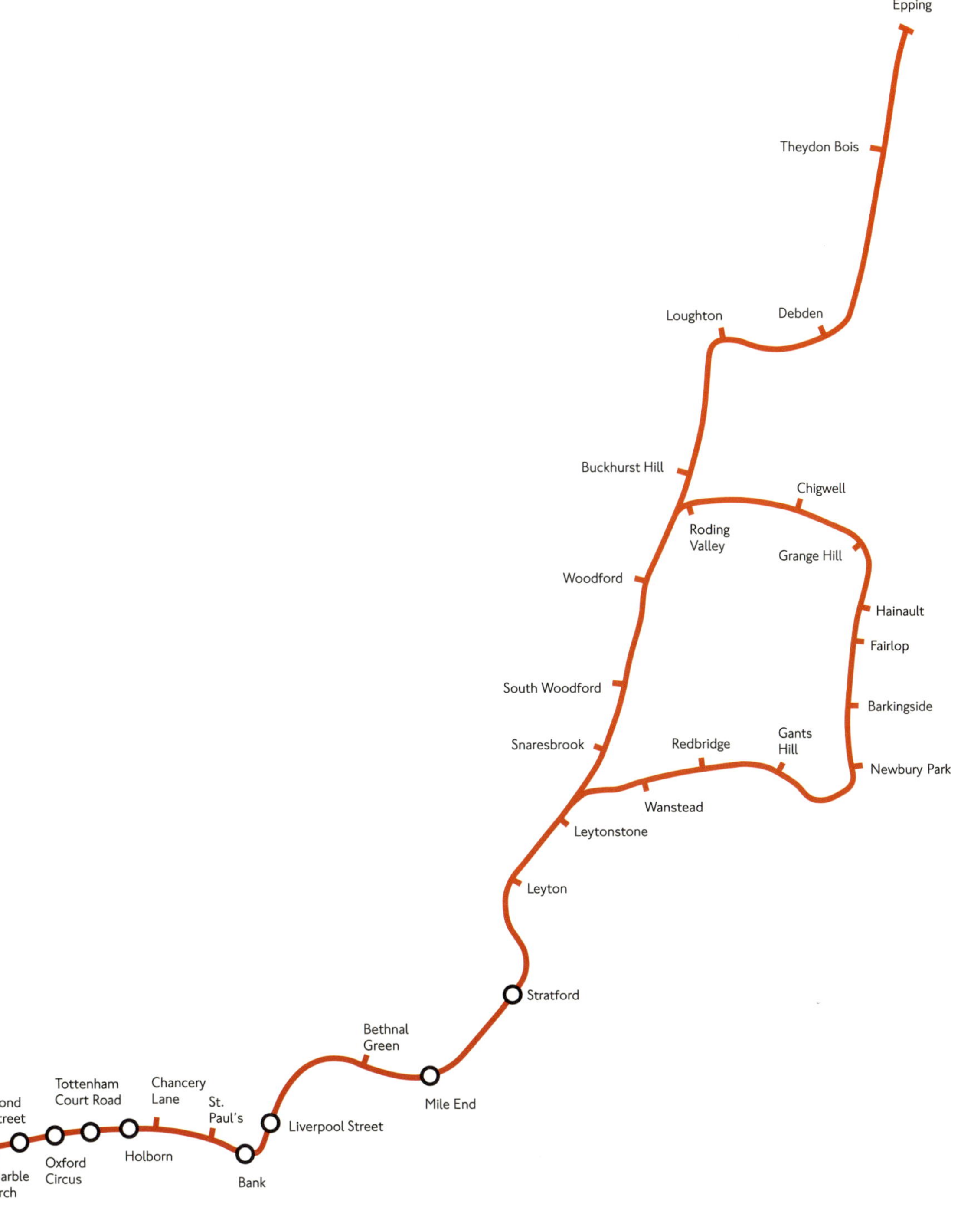

Geographic map of the Central line.

Introduction

The Central London Railway (CLR) was opened by HRH Albert Edward Prince of Wales on 27 June 1900.* In its initial incarnation, the line connected Shepherd's Bush to Bank, covering approximately five and a half miles through the centre of London.[1] Several proposed, but failed, extensions to the line illustrate how its current shape has become intertwined with the identity of the city. In 1902, for example, it was suggested that the CLR should operate as a loop from Shepherd's Bush to Liverpool Street via Hammersmith, Hyde Park Corner and Mansion House. In 1912, it was proposed that the line should run through Chiswick and Richmond. The difficulty of trying to imagine this proposal or any other than the line's current configuration is evidence of the extent to which our transport system defines our experience of the city. The influence of the transport network on the social, political and economic state of London is demonstrated in the unexpected relationship between the opening of the CLR and the decline of the umbrella industry: gentlemen who had once relied on umbrellas to protect their silk hats while travelling on open-top buses no longer needed them. Providing a safe, clean and affordable means of crossing the busiest sections of the capital, the CLR immediately altered the daily lives of Londoners and changed the fabric of the city.

Over the course of a century, the Central line—as it became known in 1933—has expanded, stations have been remodelled and the infrastructure has been modernised. Today, the line connects 49 stations and spans 74 kilometres (46 miles), from west to east London. It is the longest line in the London Underground network and serves an average of 792,548 passengers a day. Coloured a bold red on the Tube map, it is London's central artery, channelling workers,

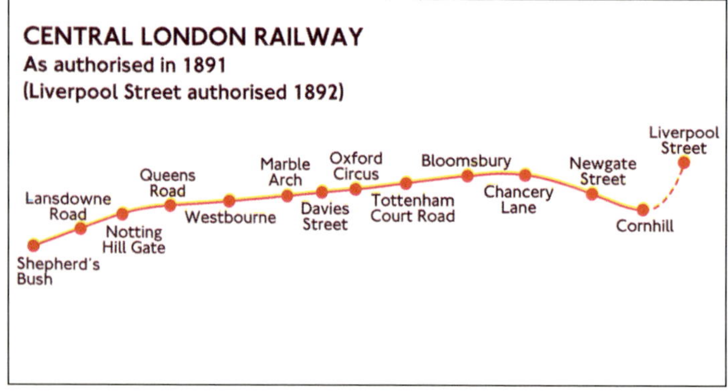

London Underground map

shoppers, commuters, students and tourists from the leafy suburbs of northwest London, through Westfield shopping centre, past the headquarters of the BBC and the site of the 1908 Olympic Games, into central London, and out again into the green spaces of Epping, via Hackney and the new Olympic and Paralympic site at Stratford. What operational demands confront the line today? How does one line provide a standard service for a city in which over 300 languages are spoken? How can station staff at Hanger Lane respond to an emergency in Hainault that will affect the service of the line? The physical expanse of the Central line, the number of staff employed by it and the immense diversity of its users were the starting points for curatorial conversations about the Central line series. Taking these challenges into consideration, the themes of communication, connection and exchange emerged, and the invited artists were asked to create new work in response to these themes and the context of the line itself.

Art and railways are not obvious companions. When the Central London first opened in 1900, drivers were expected to work ten-hour shifts with no meal breaks.[2] Obviously, much has changed since then, but working on a railway is still a demanding job, with time frequently spent alone, underground or in high-stress situations. With all this as a backdrop, it can be difficult for Art on the Underground staff and station staff to get to know one another, and to engage in a commissioning process together. It is a challenge for artists to understand the complexity of London Underground as an organisation, let alone to consider it their gallery or studio. But these challenges are just a few examples of the obstacles that confront an organisation that employs over 30,000 people working in such varied and different capacities, from heritage management to lift engineering. In 2009, the artist and writer Sarah Butler undertook a six-month residency on the Central line to collaborate with staff, resulting in a body of new writing. The project exposed what art does time and time again: it opened up new channels of communication, forged new relationships and offered opportunities to reflect on familiar and day-to-day experiences.

The project set a precedent for the Central line series. In 2011, Art on the Underground, working in partnership with Barbican Art Gallery, Chisenhale Gallery, Create Festival and the Whitechapel Gallery invited Ruth Ewan to make a new work involving young people. Working alongside Ewan were composer Kerry Andrew and poet Evlynn Sharp, who each brought their own skills and experience of communication to the work. The resulting project, *A LOCK IS A GATE*, involved 40 members of the Laburnum Boat Club youth project in Hackney, who created an album of experimental songs, a book of drawings, posters for the Central line and artwork for Bethnal Green Tube station. The opportunity to work with Laburnum arose through the personal contact of a Group Station Manager on the Central line. The project became a conduit for conversations between the artists, young people, station staff and the Art on the Underground programme. *A LOCK IS A GATE* then manifested itself in an artwork on a new site for Art on the Underground, an escalator frieze at Bethnal Green station.

In a similar way, Michael Landy's *Acts of Kindness* created new opportunities for dialogue amongst staff, and between staff and customers by bringing art into previously uncharted spaces on the London Underground network. Landy invited members of the public to submit stories of kindness that they had witnessed or experienced on the Tube. Interested in the small acts of kindness that often go unnoticed, he wanted to place the stories in unusual places across the Central line, so that passengers could chance upon them as they might chance upon everyday acts of kindness. In this way, the project established new ways of communicating with, and soliciting stories from, customers. In addition, *Acts of Kindness* seemed to tap into a zeitgeist: in the face of economic doom and gloom, Londoners were ready to share their stories of generosity between strangers. The project received a large amount of media attention and as a result, over 700 customers participated in contributing stories.

In its early days, the Central London Railway was known as the "the Twopenny Tube". Distinct from other modes of transport, the Central London Railway had no first and second class fares, but offered a flat rate for any distance of travel. And it was cheaper than the horse-drawn buses above ground. For the first time, Londoners from all walks of life would spend their journeys alongside one another. The London Underground remains one of the few areas of urban space in which total strangers are regularly thrust together in close quarters for a definite period of time. It is this sense of a temporary community that inspired a number of projects in the Central line series. For Landy, community meant revealing, and celebrating, conviviality amongst passengers. For Ewan, it was about drawing out young people's experiences through different means of expression to create new artwork. In addition, in working with the Laburnum Boat Club, Ewan provided young people with an opportunity to give something back to their community, evidenced in the large, radiant frieze created for Bethnal Green Underground station. Landy and Ewan celebrate diversity in community by giving one platform to a rich mix of participants. For Ewan, the possibility of offering a group of young people the chance to express a part of their individual identity, as a collective, was a significant aspect of the project.

The importance of community and civic responsibility were also starting points for a project by Bob and Roberta Smith and Tim Newton. Pursuing a long-term interest in public space, tapping into current conversations about David Cameron's notion of the "Big

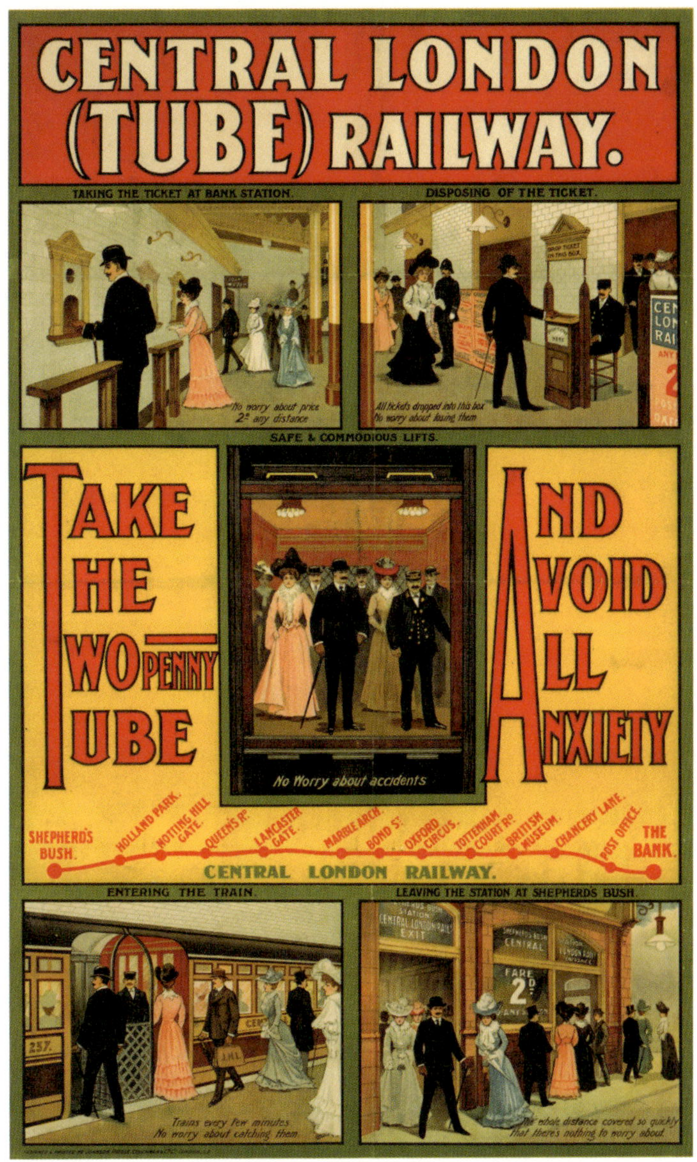

Poster advertising the Central London Railway, later known as the Central line.

Society" and reflecting upon recent large-scale municipal activities such as the street parties that surrounded the Royal Wedding in 2011 and the Diamond Jubilee in 2012, Bob and Roberta Smith began by thinking about the meaning of community. Considering the context of Stratford as the site of the London 2012 Olympic and Paralympic Park, Smith and Newton were inspired to look back at the ideals upon which the Olympic Games were founded. Revived in 1896 by the French aristocrat Pierre de Coubertin, the Olympic Games were, in many ways, borne out of an attempt to find a response to the violence and conflict of the nineteenth century. For Coubertin, sport was a way of advancing and promoting peace.

The film imagines a fictional meeting between Coubertin, and the German theorist Hannah Arendt. Using humour and an absurdist style to convey the story, *Who is Community?* interrogates what it means to participate in a community, and how freedom is connected to public space. Smith and Newton suggest that the celebration of public space and community is necessary to maintain peace and freedom. Produced and encountered in the context of the London 2012 Olympics and Paralympics Games, and commissioned by Art on the Underground, *Who is Community?* offers a unique perspective from which to consider both the development, impact and legacy of the Olympic Games, and the importance of shared space.

With huge advancements in communication technology over the last century, and particularly in recent decades, the notion of a community, and our basic assumptions about the nature of communication, have shifted. Online communities and virtual interactions are the norm. Naturally, these changing conditions influenced a number of projects in the Central line series. Landy prompted the people of London to submit their stories of kindness via a web portal. Anna Barham's *WHITE CITY* utilised Quick Response (QR) codes as a starting point for the project. These graphic-data storage devices are a bridge between the real and virtual worlds, taking the user from one to the other via an application that is downloadable on a smartphone. In Barham's project, a series of text and video works are accessed through QR codes that are embedded within posters specially designed by the artist.

Alice Channer's *Hard Metal Body* explores material in a post-industrial world. Investigating the interface between human and non-human materials, Channer created a new work for the long expanse of space alongside an escalator at Notting Hill Underground station. The project comprises a number of ellipses that are detailed imprints of elastic waistbands from clothing. The artwork is an attempt to create an exchange between the artist's own soft body and the hard metal surfaces of the Tube's underground infrastructure. In doing so, Channer tries to locate the position of the body in a post-industrial, technologically advanced society.

The conundrum of communication technology is that while improvements have made interacting easier, cheaper, faster and more frequent, online social and professional networking platforms, text-messaging and emailing are often poor conveyers of meaning, emotion and innuendo. The subtleties of language and the art of expression are falling prey to short-hand text-speak, immediate responses and distancing modes of transmission. Curiously, the Central line once doubled as a parcels delivery service, between the years 1911–17. Today, the idea of "snail mail" and handwritten letters is a fading concept. However, the inadequacy of communication, is not only the by-product of technological advancements. In *WHITE CITY*, Barham reconnoitres the construction of meaning through language, whose malleable aspects she explores by means of anagrams. In many ways, Barham's work is like a code that needs to be cracked, revealing a network of references, allusions and associations, and in this case, all via a QR code that she has purposefully distorted. The idea of unlocking or decoding meaning is succinctly put forth in Ewan's employment of the dual metaphorical meanings of 'lock', both as a prohibitive device and as an entranceway to allow a boat to pass onto different levels of water. The intricacy of language and text emerged as an important aspect of the Central line series, and remains a significant facet of communication in the public realm.

In the following pages, each project in the Central line series is represented by an explanatory text, alongside images and contextualising information about the project. The book also includes three commissioned essays that explore some of the themes brought to light by the artworks in this series. Contributing writers, who are all interested in, and respected voices on, these subjects, were asked to respond to these themes in an oblique way, drawing upon their areas of expertise and current research, rather than specifically referencing the artworks in the Central line series. Mark Pagel, Professor of Evolutionary Biology at the University of Reading and author of *Wired for Culture*, 2012, has written on the theme of language, pointing out the dazzling array of languages spoken around the world (there are approximately 7,000 mutually unintelligible languages), the difficulties that language presents for communication and the way in which it is so intrinsically linked to our identity. Federico Campagna, a political and literary activist who works with Verso Books, takes up the theme of community, challenging the utopian aspirations upon which membership is so often grounded. And finally, the publication includes a reprinted text by Kazys Varnelis, Director of the Network Architecture Lab at the Columbia University Graduate School of Architecture, Planning, and Preservation. Taking network theory as a point of departure, the essay reflects upon shifting patterns of communication and notions of public space in the new digital era. We hope that this rich consortium of contributions provides a broad and interesting context from which to approach the projects in the series.

Charlotte Bonham-Carter,
Curator, Art on the Underground

---

* The Central line was known as Central London Railway (or Central London) until the new London Passenger Transport Board began to operate on 1 July 1933, and the Central London Railway ceased to have an effective separate existence, although it was not legally wound up until 10 March 1939.

1 Bruce, Graeme and Desmond F Croome, *The Twopenny Tube*, Middlesex: Capital Transport Publishing, 1996, p. 5.
2 Bruce, *The Twopenny Tube*, p. 18.

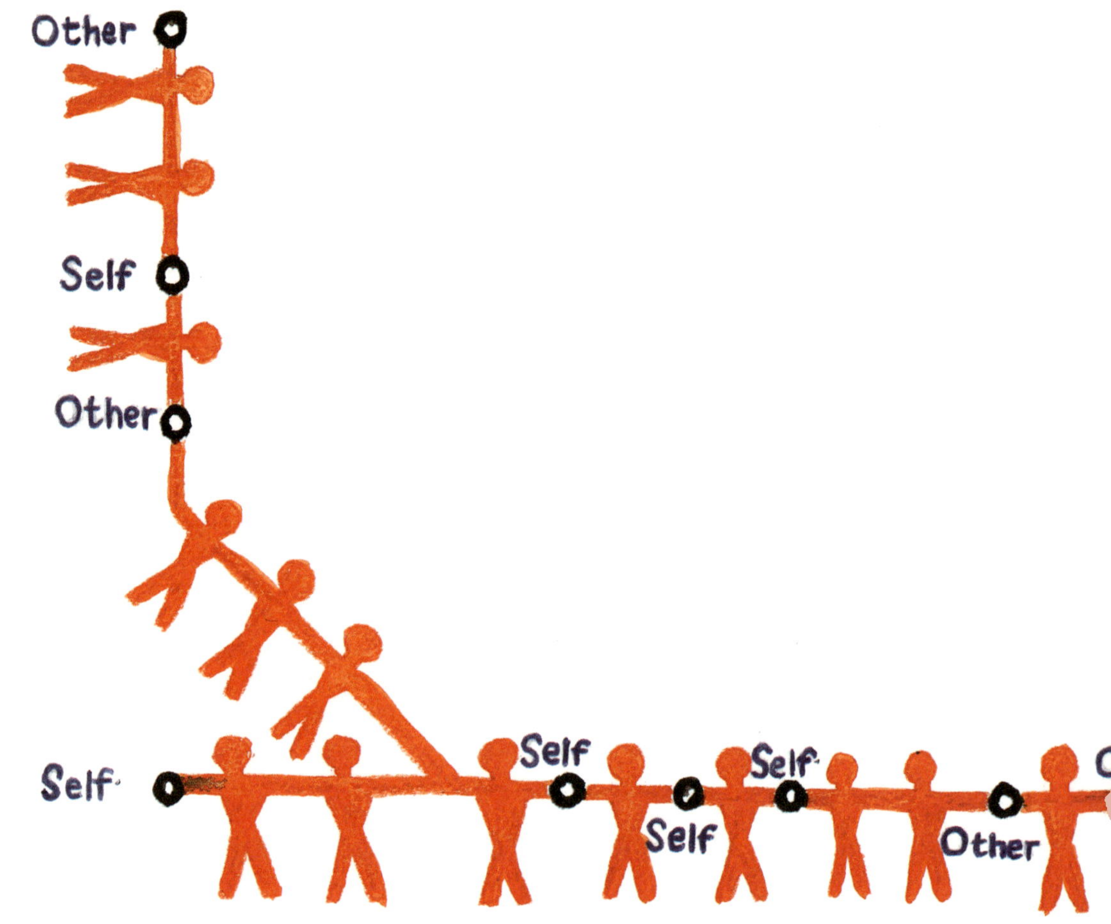

Other
Self
Other
Self
Self
Self
Self
Other

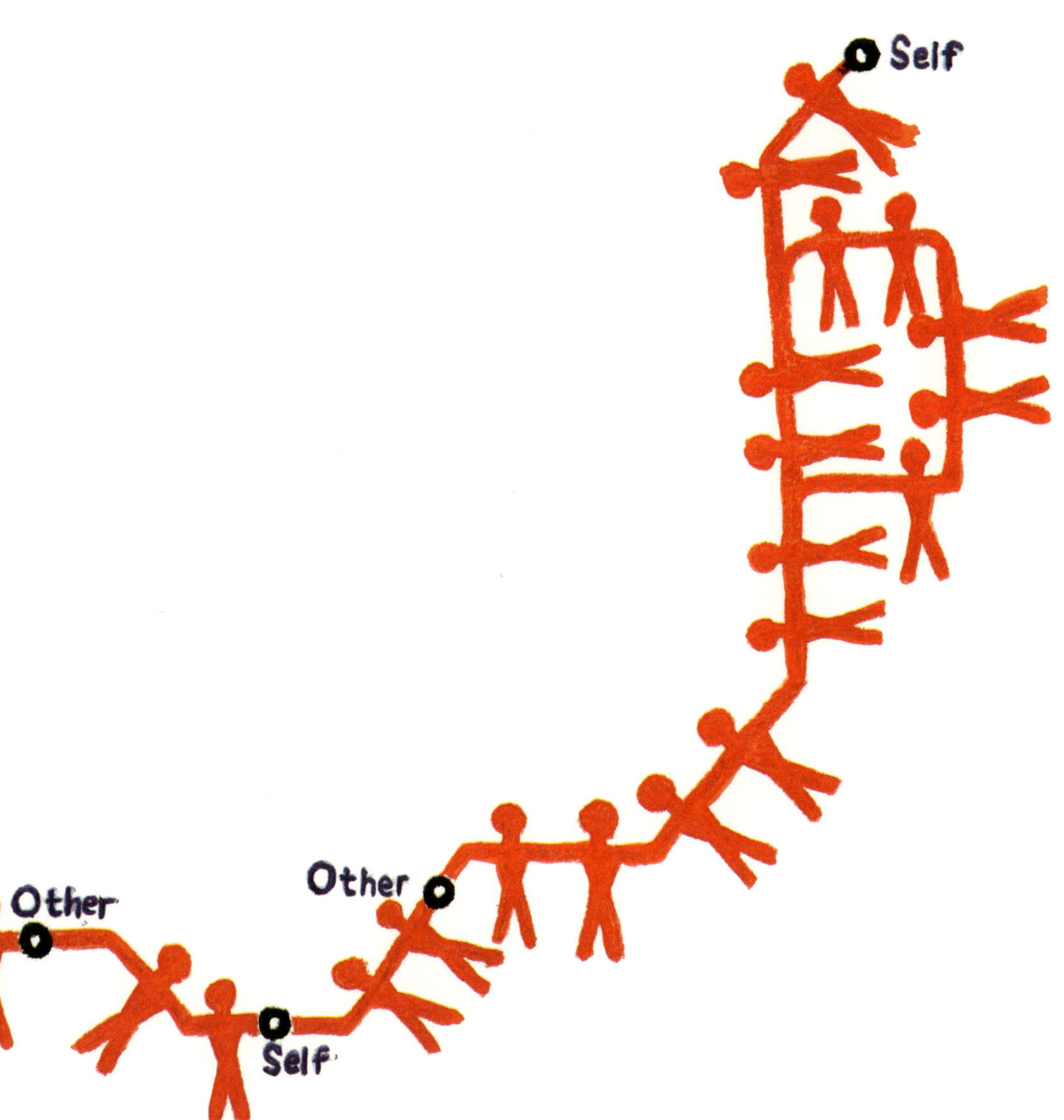

Self
Other
Other
Self

Communication—
Just a Small Part of Language

Here is a remarkable fact about humans: we speak approximately 7,000 mutually unintelligible languages around the world. That is, we have 7,000 different ways of saying "Good morning", or "What's for dinner?". To put this number in perspective, 7,000 is more different languages for a single mammal species—for that is what we are—than there are mammal species. In London alone, between 250 to 300 different languages are spoken, making it perhaps the world's most linguistically diverse city.

But having so many different languages means that humans are perhaps the only species whose members cannot all communicate with each other. Why would the only species to employ language use their system of communication in such a way that it effectively cuts them off from other members of their own species? The answer seems to be that language is about far more than mere communication. And London's vast linguistic diversity is a living example.

One of the best-known theories for the diversity of human languages is a creation myth. According to the bible story of the Tower of Babel, humans developed the conceit that they could construct a tower that would take them all the way to Heaven. Angered at this attempt to usurp His control, God destroyed the tower. To ensure that it could not be rebuilt, He confused the workers by giving them different languages—leading to the amusing irony that our languages exist to prevent us from communicating.

The reason why we have many different languages might seem obvious. As humans drifted around the world after migrating out of Africa around 60,000 years ago, their languages naturally diverged as they lived in different places. We see this happening today in the differing accents of British, Australian and American speakers of English. But there might be more to the Tower of Babel myth than initially meets the eye (or ear), because the greatest diversity of human societies and languages emerges not where people are most spread out, but where they are most closely packed together. Take the case of Papua New Guinea. That relatively small island land mass—only slightly larger than the American state of Texas—hosts 800–1,000 distinct languages, or around 15 per cent of all languages spoken on the planet. Incredible as it sounds, there are parts of northeast coastal Papua New Guinea where a new language can be found every few miles. I once met a Papuan man from that area and asked him if this could be true. He replied, "Oh no, they're far closer together than that."

Of course, unlike in Papua New Guinea, London's many languages didn't evolve there but were brought in by immigrants. And yet, these distinct languages are maintained rather than all blending into one.

This is all the more remarkable in London, with its winding and highly interconnected underground system that is constantly moving and mixing people together, creating a vast and continuously changing public space of murmuring and overheard voices. Central line trains alone are estimated to travel over 7,800 miles per day, clanging back and forth from East to West, carrying tens of thousands of people along the lines that connect its 47 stations and span the geographic, cultural and linguistic divisions of London.

This tendency for languages to retain their separate identities even when their speakers are effectively living on top of one another is something they share with biological species. One of the best-known trends of ecology is Rapaport's Rule, which describes the great increase in the number of different species as one moves from the cold polar regions to the warmer Equatorial habitats. It turns out that the same trend is true of human language groups. For example, around 500 different Native American tribes have been documented as inhabiting North America prior to contact with Europeans. Just as with different biological species, many of these different language groups are found in the southern latitudes of North America compared to only a handful at extreme northern latitudes, and this despite the far greater land mass in the North.

It might not be surprising that few mammal species and few language groups are found in the polar regions—after all, the landscape is harsh. And the large numbers of different species in the tropics might just reflect the variety and richness of resources in that environment. But, unlike other animals, humans are all the same species. So why are there so many different language groups in these southern regions instead of one large cooperative society of people all talking to each other?

One answer is that humans seem to have an innate tendency to form into small tribal groups, and we use our languages as explicit and highly tuned markers of tribal identity. In my book *Wired for Culture*, 2012, I describe anthropological accounts of tribal elders who decide, together with their people, to change their languages—and with immediate effect—for no other reason than to distinguish themselves from neighbouring tribes. One tribe of Selepet speakers in Papua New Guinea reversed all of its masculine and feminine nouns—so he would become she, or him would become her and *vice versa*. Another Papua New Guinean group decided to change its word for "no" from *bia* to *bune*. One can only sympathise with someone who had been away hunting for a few days while this important decision was taken.

Many of the spelling differences between British and American English—such as the dropping of the 'u' in words like colour and honour—arose almost overnight when the American educator and compiler of dictionaries Noah Webster (1758–1843) produced the first *American Dictionary of the English Language*. In preparing that work he insisted that "as an independent nation, our honor requires us to have a system of our own, in language as well as government". To Webster at least, the spelling of words as a way of marking out a distinct identity was as important as the philosophical issues that lay behind the American War of Independence.

Even in our modern world, we use language to construct and then advertise our identities. The rapid spread of so-called "estuarine English" a few years ago (think of the British television personality Jonathan Ross) is a good example, but so is our almost obsessive awareness of differing regional accents. On top of this, though, we use language strategically to adopt multiple identities throughout any given day, depending upon whom we are seated next to, asking directions of, or ordering something from. Linguists call this "code-switching". Without even thinking, we adjust our language to the perceived demands of our listeners, or we strategically adjust it in ways that broadcast what we want others to think about us.

What does the future hold for languages? The increasing interconnectedness of the modern world owing to the internet, mass communication and transport is having a homogenising effect on language and culture. Some years ago, in a remote part of Tanzania, I was stopped while attempting to speak Swahili to a local person who held up his hand and said, "My English is better than your Swahili." It isn't just that my Swahili is limited, but that everyone seems to be speaking English, whether it be freedom fighters in Libya and Syria, or Chinese students on the streets of Beijing.

It's likely that everyone in London experiences a 'Tanzania moment' every day and in most parts of the city. Just go into your local Starbucks where, while standing in the queue, you are likely to overhear people for whom English is not their first language ordering coffee from *baristas* for whom English is also not their first language, and yet everyone will be speaking in English, or at least a simplified local variety—code-switching again. So, in spite of our tendencies to maintain our linguistic identities, there is pressure for everyone to speak as the local majority does. Because of this, the rate in the loss of minority languages now greatly exceeds the production of new languages around the world. Currently around 30–50 languages are disappearing every year. It isn't that speakers of these languages are dying. This is the inevitable effect of people abandoning their native languages for the majority languages spoken nearby.

The rate in the loss of minority languages now equals or exceeds (as a percentage of the total) the loss of biological species through destruction of habitat and climate change. Already, just ten languages (Chinese, Spanish, English, Bengali, Hindi, Portuguese, Russian, Japanese, French and German) out of the 7,000 or so living languages account for around 40 per cent of the world's seven billion speakers, while the majority of languages have very few speakers at all, often fewer than 1,000.

Inevitably—although it might be a long way off—everyone in the world will speak a single language; it's already the case that English is nearly every non-English speaker's second language. Happily, though, there is no reason to believe that this loss of linguistic diversity means that the world is losing unique styles of thought; contrary to a widely held belief, our languages do not determine how we think, just the language we think in. But the loss of languages often does coincide with the loss of cultural diversity. And this leaves us with one of the fundamental contradictions of modern life—that the very cultural diversity that can make great cities like London or New York enjoyable and interesting places in which to live seems to be ebbing away as migrants adopt local languages and customs to ease their passage through daily life. This is something to think about the next time you find yourself standing in one of those coffee queues.

Mark Pagel

Mark Pagel is a Fellow of the Royal Society, Professor of Evolutionary Biology at the University of Reading and External Professor at the renowned Santa Fe Institute in the USA. He has travelled the world, studying evolution and the spread of cultures from the Chalbi Desert in Kenya to Tanzania and Zanzibar, and remote Oceania. He is the editor-in-chief of the award winning *Oxford Encyclopaedia of Evolution*, 2006 and co-author of *The Comparative Method in Evolutionary Biology*, 1991, which is regarded as a classic, as well as the author of articles in *Science*, *Nature* and other journals. His new book *Wired for Culture* was published in February 2012.

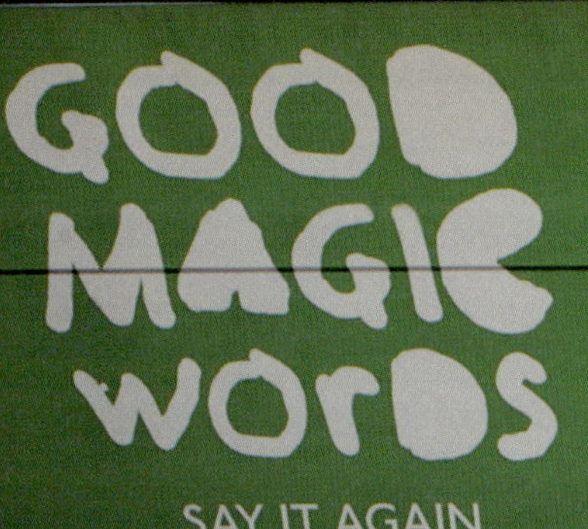

GOOD
MAGIC
WORDS
SAY IT AGAIN
GOOD
MAGIC
WORDS
Live forever machine
Equal Money Machine
Water machine
Food Machine

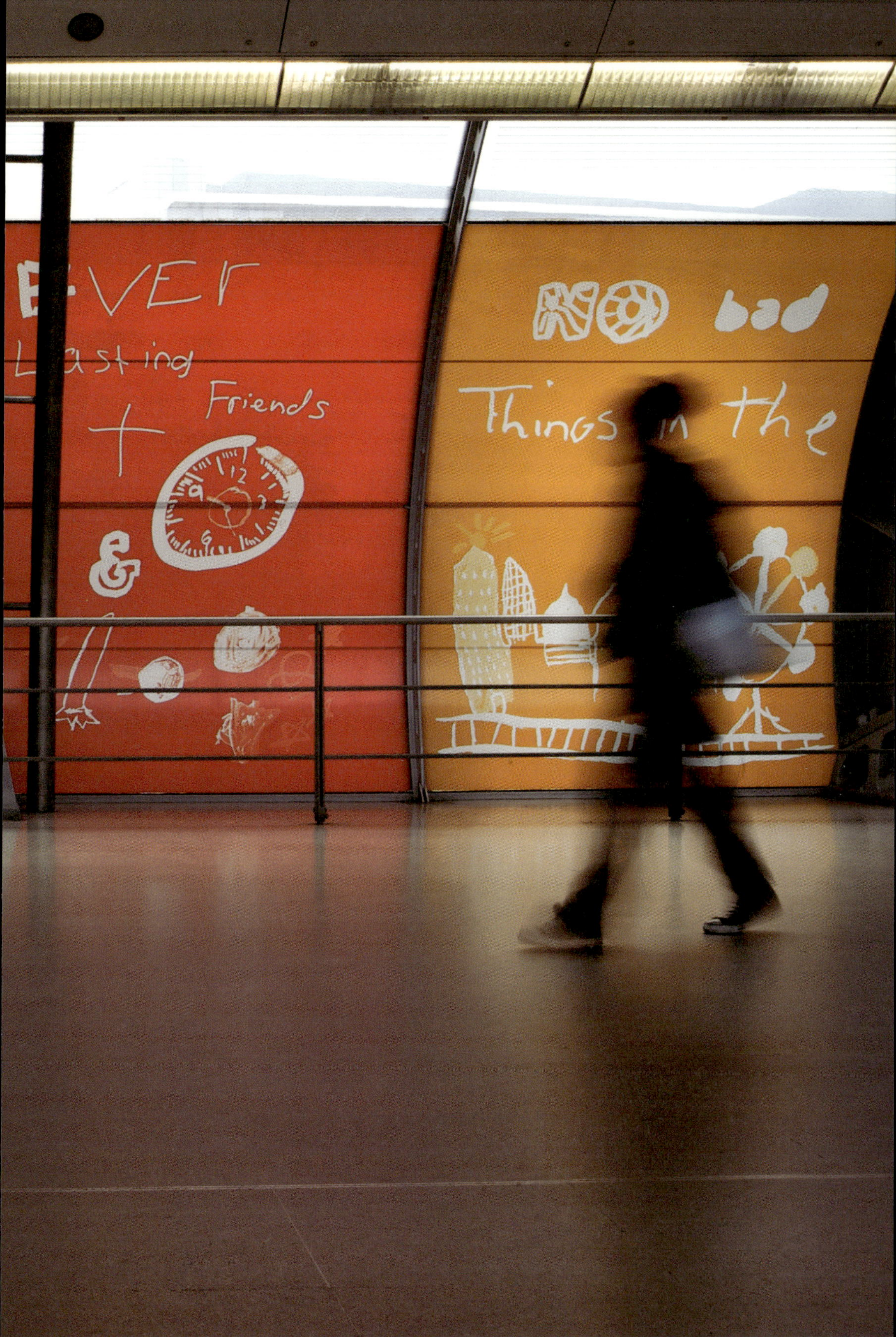

EVEr
Lasting
Friends
NO bad
Things in the

Community is dead—Long live community

Many voices advocate the urgent need to think beyond civilisation. It is not just an abstract claim. From several points of view—environmental, economic and military—the world as we know it is on the brink of an epochal catastrophe. We should understand catastrophe according to the etymological meaning of the word *katastrephein*: "to overturn, to come to an end". Comprehended as a sudden and general transformation, catastrophe is clearly knocking on our doors. How can we imagine the catastrophe of our lives outside and beyond the familiar context to which we are accustomed?

When we look at our position in the contemporary world, we see how it is essentially limited by two categories of boundary: the social and the natural (or, more correctly, biological). We can understand as a biological limit that which is imposed on us by the conformation of our bodies, by their 'natural' abilities and faults. On the other hand, social limitations are those imposed by the manmade structures and contexts within which we happen to live.

Despite the claims of modern science, biological limits present themselves as highly rigid. The developments of medicine in the last centuries have helped humans to bring themselves closer to the boundaries of their possibilities, but they have not—and they cannot—deliver their promise of allowing humans to go beyond them, or to 'evolve' into the new and, under certain perspectives, superior life form of the android. Differently from biological limits, those imposed by society are extremely fluid. Their arbitrariness is equal to that of nature, but it relates to the decisive will of the humans who establish them in the first place. However, this fluidity is hardly ever reflected in the way in which societal structures and boundaries present themselves to a member of the human consortia.

The paradox between the constitutive fluidity and practical rigidity of societal structures is particularly evident in the case of some of the most immediate social boundaries that confront a person: belonging to one or many communities. The idea of community presents itself, in theory, as the 'natural' expression of an association of humans. Community is nothing but the 'innocent' excess that derives from the union of a plurality of people. Often, this excess finds its material form in the shape of a flag, a cause, an ideal, or simply a name. While some communities are created voluntarily—for example, communities based on taste in music or political ideas—the vast majority pre-exist for most of their members. It is true, for example, in ethnic, national or territorial communities. In either case, however, the functioning of the community is the same: the excess deriving from the union of a plurality rises above the members of the communities and presents itself to them both as a horizon of possibilities, as a goal and as a normative element. If the community was originally created as a tool aimed at satisfying the specific needs of its members, the moment it installs itself as a normative and utopian element above the heads of its members, the set of priorities of its functioning is changed. The interest in which the members of a community are called to act is not their petty, egoistic individual interest, but that of the community. The life that all the members of a community are supposed to nurture and protect is not their mortal, fragile, expendable life, but the immortal existence of the community. The king is dead, long live the king.

People are expected to identify as members of their community, and to act accordingly. The failure to do so is clearly perceived by the other members—but often equally by members of other communities—as an act of treason, occasionally subject to punishment. This state of subjection of the individual towards his/her community has been famously questioned by feminist critiques, in reference to the community of the family. While some commentators limited themselves to pointing out the repressive characteristics of the patriarchal family, others, more radically, pushed the argument to the point of questioning the structure of the family altogether. Regardless of the gender of those who are in power within it, the very structure of the family produces alienation in its members and locks them into a state of minority and subjection. As is equally clear in the case of as large a community as that of the State, the reforms that bring one or the other part into a position of hegemony within the community do not change the basic fact that the community itself is the ultimate element that all members are called upon to protect and honour. The history of revolutions and repressions of the past century leaves little doubt about this, especially in reference to the State as a community. It makes no great difference who makes a bid to take power within the State, as long as the State itself is not compromised.

We can understand this difference between competitors within the State community and downright 'traitors'—that is, those who threaten the existence of the State as such—if we observe the category of political imprisonment and its differences from that of common criminality. During all the numerous political upheavals and attempted revolutions of the past century, all those who were imprisoned by the government they opposed demanded to be recognised as political prisoners. The reason for this demand lies, on the one hand, on the advantages granted to political prisoners by international agreements on human rights. On the other hand, however, the reason for such a focus on the category of political

imprisonments derives from the urgency of differentiating oneself
from criminals on the basis of one's respect for the institution of
the State as such. If the criminal is a threat to the State—and not
just to a government—the political rebel is a defender of the State,
and an enemy of the specific government of that time.

How can we use the category of the criminal/traitor in an attempt
to make a catastrophe of our life as we know it, or to envision a
possible outcome for the catastrophes that are already underway? If
we assume that the biological boundaries imposed on us by physical
nature are fixed, we should focus our attention on the social limits
within which humans are restricted as members of their communities.
In an attempt to imagine life after—or beyond—civilisation, the
struggle to escape such boundaries is of the utmost importance,
since these very boundaries are the inner structures upon which
civilisation rests. In fact, we could understand 'civilisation' at its core
as a social system of idealist normativity and repression.

By moving away from the structure of the community, however, we
would not be doing without the possibility of an association of free
people. The desire for a life that is unrestrained by idealist, societal
bonds does not necessarily translate into the isolation of the hermit.
Brought together by their need for company or by the necessities of
life, individuals are still able to compose associations that do not
transcend their individual status and their mortal lives. Seen from this
perspective, a union of individuals—or, to borrow the words of the
philosopher Max Stirner, a "union of egoists"—is an association
of people that is created with the sole function of pursuing the
objectives of its members.[1] Differently from a community, such a
group does not exist as separate from its members, and nor can it
survive their existential and biological dynamics. Similarly, nobody can
be born within a union of egoists, since the assignation at birth of an
individual to one of these groups would resemble the impossibility
perceived by the Anabaptists in the fifteenth and sixteenth centuries
in reference to the act of baptising an oblivious baby: as they put it,
it would count as much as "washing a dog".

Understood as a union that is entirely dependent on and functional
to its members, this type of association would indeed be describable
as a union of criminals or of traitors. Such unions would represent a
truly atheistic type of association, devoid of any central abstraction,
flag or ideal around which their members could congregate and swear
their loyalty and obedience. Exactly because of this utter
submissiveness to the desires and needs of their members, these
unions would excel in times of urgency, such as those that seem to
be ahead of us with the impending dissolution of the contemporary
world order. And yet, the urgency that underlines the necessity for

this movement beyond communities can already be found in an honest and deep understanding of the natural, biological limits to which our mortal bodies are subjected.

If we face our position within the natural world as necessarily and utterly precarious, constantly threatened by death and ultimately pointing towards a death devoid of rebirth or afterlife, we cannot but admit the urgency of taking possession of our lives and of all the pleasure and joy that can be contained in them. As the Enlightenment philosopher Giacomo Leopardi remarked, nature acts towards us like an unloving step-mother, constantly ready to take away from us what we have.[2] Against this bleak scenario and this pessimistic understanding, human individuals are called by the very fragility of their condition to refrain from sacrificing the little precious time and energy they have in the maintenance and worshipping of abstract excesses such as the flags or names of their supposed communities.

It is with the skillfulness of the criminal, and not with the rebelliousness of the martyr, that we are called to live by our mortal fragility. It is the intelligence of the traitor not the blind heroism of the patriot that can guide us along the dimly lit path that stretches like our lives through the infinite darkness of nature.

Federico Campagna

Federico Campagna is an anarchist writer. He is one of the founders of the online journal *Through Europe* (www.th-rough.eu). He is the editor of the forthcoming volume *What We Are Fighting For* (Pluto Press, UK) and of the philosophical anthology of Autonomia thinker Franco Berardi Bifo (Il Saggiatore, Italy). Born in Italy, he currently resides in London.

---

1 Stirner, Max, *The Ego and Its Own*, David Leopold ed, Cambridge: Cambridge University Press, 1995.

2 Leopardi, Giacomo, "The Broom or the Flower of the Desert", in J G Nichols ed, *The Canti*, Manchester: Carcanet Press, 1995, p. 141.

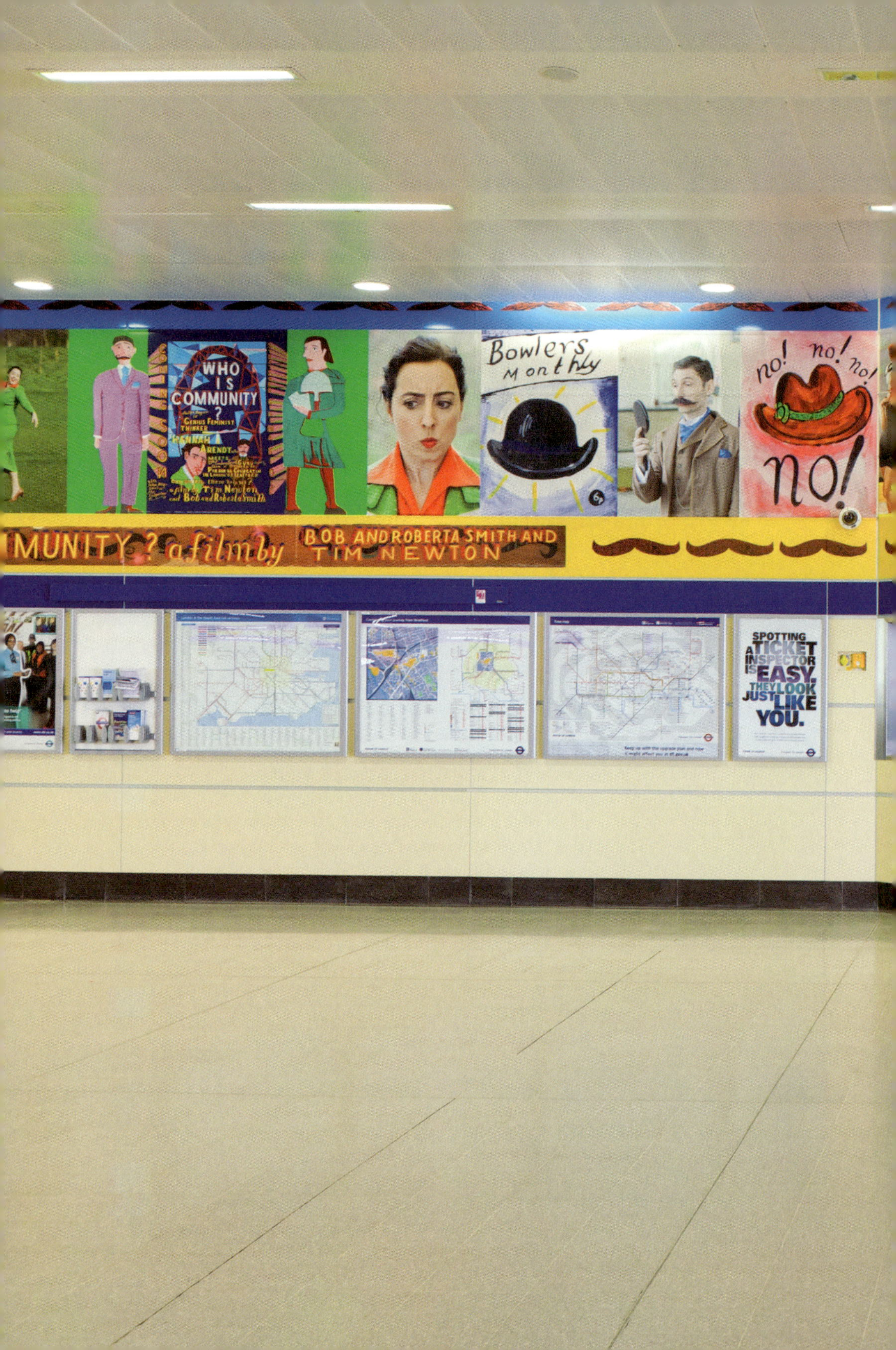

WHO IS COMMUNITY ?
GENIUS FEMINIST THINKER
HANNAH ARENDT
Bowlers Monthly
no! no! no!
no!
MUNITY ? a film by BOB AND ROBERTA SMITH AND TIM NEWTON
SPOTTING A TICKET INSPECTOR IS EASY. THEY LOOK JUST LIKE YOU.

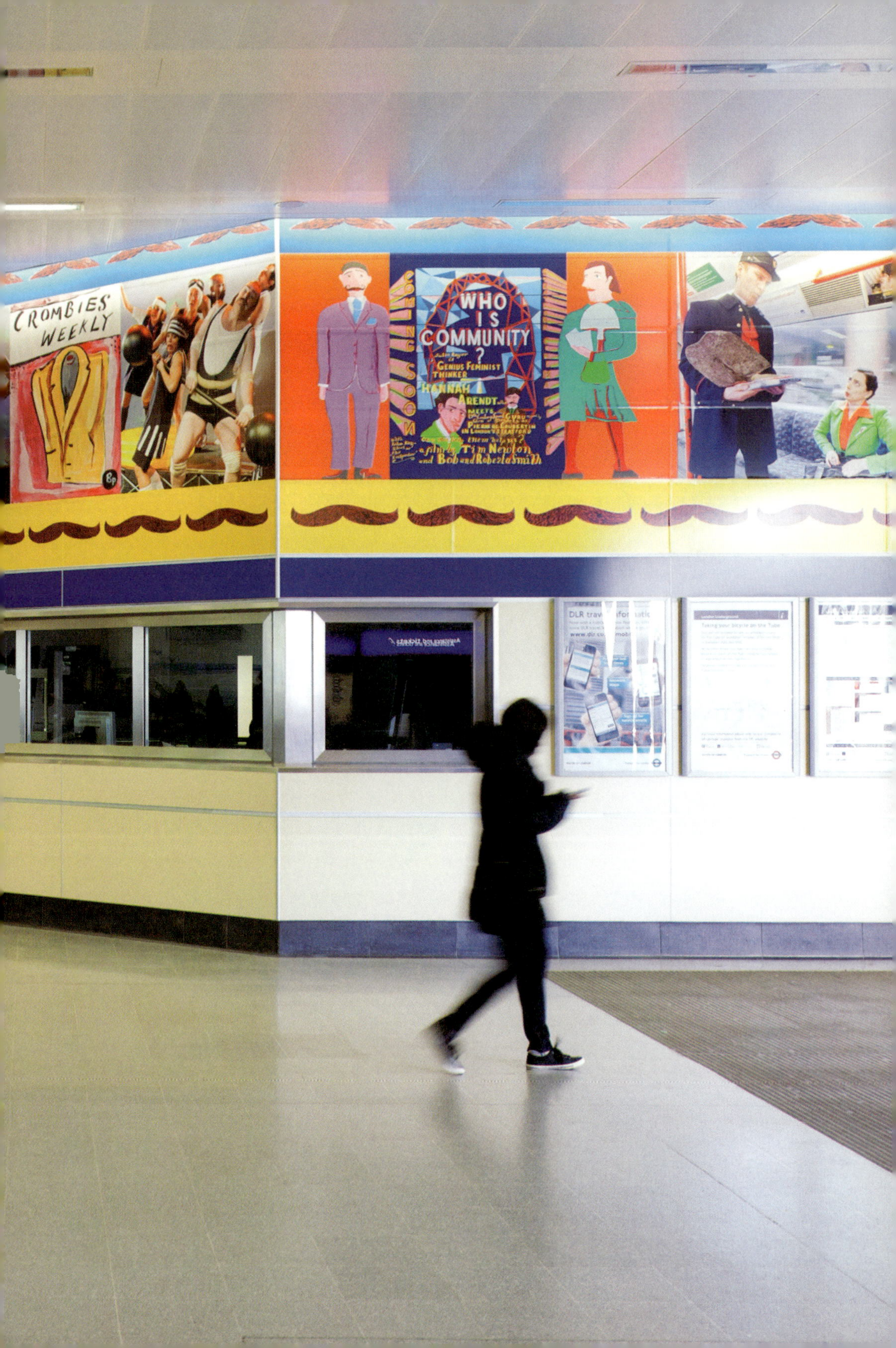

CROMBIES' WEEKLY
8p
WHO IS COMMUNITY ?
GENIUS FEMINIST THINKER
HANNAH ARENDT
MEETS
PIERRE de COUBERTIN
a film by Tim Newton
and Bob and Roberta Smith
DLR travel information
www.dlr.co.uk/mobile
Taking your bicycle on the Tube

The Meaning of Network Culture

In network theory, a node's relationship to other networks is more important than its own uniqueness. Similarly, today we situate ourselves less as individuals and more as the product of multiple networks composed of both humans and things. This is easily demonstrated through some everyday examples. First, take the way the youth of today affirm their identities. Teens create pages on social networking sites such as MySpace and Facebook. On these pages they list their interests as a set of hyperlinked keywords directing the reader to others with similar interests. Frequently, page creators use algorithms to express (and thereby create) their identities—for example, through a Web page that, in return for responses to a set of questions, suggests what 'chick flick' character the respondent is. At the most reductive, these algorithms take the form of simple questionnaires to be filled out and posted wholesale on one's page. Beyond making such links, posting comments about others and soliciting such comments can become an obsessive activity. Affirming one's own identity today means affirming the identity of others in a relentless potlatch. Blogs operate similarly. If they appear to be the public expression of an individual voice, in practice many blogs consist of material poached from other blogs coupled with pointers to more in the same network—for example trackbacks (notifications that a blogger has posted comments about a blog post on another blogger's blog) or blogrolls (the long lists of blogs that frequently border blog pages). With social bookmarking services such as del. icio.us or the social music platform last.fm, even the commentary that accompanies blog posts can disappear and the user's public face turns into a pure collection of links. Engaging in telepresence by sending SMS messages to friends or calling family on a mobile phone has the same effect: the networked subject is constituted by networks both far and near, large and small. Like the artist, the networked self is an aggregator of information flows, a collection of links to others, a switching machine.

Along with this change in the self comes a new attitude toward privacy. Many blogs reconfigure the personal and the public, as individuals reveal details that had previously been considered private. The idea of locks on diaries today seems almost preposterous as individuals, particularly teenagers, discuss their most intimate—and illicit—details online. Meanwhile, advances in computation and networking have made it possible to store data on individuals to a greater degree than ever imaginable. As debit cards and other technologies replace cash, our actions, be they online or out on the town, leave behind a trail of information. Corporations routinely track which websites individuals visit at work. In the wake of 9/11, governments have taken to recording more and more communications traffic, even when that recording is of questionable legality. As tracking increases, advances in data-mining mean that those wishing to find information can do so more easily than ever before.

But if this degree of surveillance conjures images of George Orwell's *1984*, there has been relatively little protest. That Watergate undid Nixon seems impossible in retrospect. To some degree this is a case of what security researcher Ross Anderson calls "boiling the frog" (a frog in a pot of water doesn't notice when the temperature of the water is raised incrementally, and it boils to death). Nevertheless, it also underscores the degree to which privacy is no longer important in this culture. As the subject is increasingly less sure of where the self begins and ends, the question of what should be private and what should not also fades.

In network culture, then, the waning of the subject that began under postmodernism grows ever greater. But whereas in postmodernism, being was left in a free-floating fabric of emotional intensities, today it is found in the net. The Cartesian "I think therefore I am" dissolves in favour of an affirmation of existence through the network itself, a phantom individuality that escapes into the network, much as meaning escapes into the Derridean network of *différance*, where words are defined by other words, significance endlessly deferred in a ceaseless play of language.[1] The division between the self and the net that Manuel Castells observed a decade ago is undone.

Nor are the networks that make up the contemporary self merely networks of people. On the contrary, they are also networks between people and things. In Bruno Latour's analysis, things are not merely objects that do our bidding but are key actors in the network. As things get smarter and smarter, they are ever more likely to make up larger parts of our 'selves'. An iPod is nothing less than a portable generator of affect with which we paint our environment, creating a soundtrack to life. A Blackberry or telephone constantly receiving text messages encourages its owner to submit to a distracted state, a condition much lamented by many.[2]

It is in this context that networked publics form.[3] Apart from the loss of the self, of all the changes that network culture brings us, the reconfiguration of the public sphere is likely to be the most significant, a distinction that makes our moment altogether unlike any other in three centuries. After the Enlightenment, the public came to be understood as a realm of politics, media and culture, a site of display and debate open to every citizen while, in turn, the private was broadly understood as a realm of freedom, inwardness and individuality. The public sphere was the space in which bourgeois culture and politics played out, a theatre for bourgeois citizens to play their role in shaping and legitimating society. In its origin as a body to which the king would appear, the public is by nature a responsive, reflexive and thereby a responsible and empowered entity. Founded on the sovereign's need for approval during the contentious later years of the aristocracy (an approval that was eventually withdrawn), the public sphere served as a check on the state. In that respect, the public sphere served in the same capacity as media: at the same time as the emergence of the newspaper, the gallery, the novel, modern theatre, music and so on, the public produced voices of criticism. Even if the equation of public space and public sphere was problematic, by understanding media as a space (or conversely space as a medium), it was nevertheless possible to draw a rough link between the two.

As many theorists observed, the twentieth century was witness to a long, sustained decline in the public sphere. In Habermas' analysis, this came about due to the contamination of the public sphere by private matters, most crucially its colonisation by capital and the consequent transformation of the media from a space of discourse to a commodified realm. As media concentrated in huge conglomerates more interested in the marketing of consensus than in a theatre of deliberation, and with little use for genuinely divergent positions, mass media sought consensus in the middle ground, the political apparatus that Arthur Schlesinger called "the vital centre".Ð The model of the public became one-way, the culture industry and the political machine expecting approval or, at most, dissent within a carefully circumscribed set of choices.

Public space was not left unmolested. On the contrary, it was privatised, thoroughly colonised by capital, less a place of display for the citizen and more a theatre of consumption under high security and total surveillance.Ð In postmodernism, the condition seemed virtually total, the public privatised, reduced to opinion surveys and demographics. If there was hope for the public sphere, it came in the form of identity politics, the increasing voices of counter-publics composed of subaltern peoples (in the developed world this would have been non-whites, gays, feminists, youth, and so on), existing in tension with the dominant public. But if counterpublics could define and press their cases in their own spheres, for the broader public they were marginalised and marginalising entities, defined by their position of exclusion. Towards the end of postmodernism in the early 1990s, even identity politics became colonised, understood by marketers as another lifestyle choice among many.[6] But if this was the last capitulation of the old publics as an uncommodified realm for discourse, it was also the birth of networked publics.

Kazys Varnelis

Kazys Varnelis is the Director of the Network Architecture Lab at the Columbia University Graduate School of Architecture, Planning, and Preservation. With Robert Sumrell, he runs the non-profit architectural collective AUDC.

This essay was originally published online, at http://networkedpublics.org/book/conclusion. The essay is the third in a series of articles on the topic, Network Culture. To read the other articles, see "The Meaning of Network Culture" part one, two and four.

---

1 Derrida, Jacques, *Writing and Difference*, Chicago: University of Chicago Press, 1978.

2 Latour, Bruno, *Reassembling the Social: An Introduction to Actor-Network-Theory*, Oxford: Oxford University Press, 2005; Pearson, Patricia, "Are BlackBerry Users the New Smokers?", *USATODAY.com*, 12 December 2006.

3 Varnelis, Kazys ed, *Networked Publics*, Cambridge: The MIT Press, 2008.

4 Horkheimer, Max and Theodor W Adorno, *Dialectic of Enlightenment*, trans. John Cummings, New York: Continuum, 1991; first published in English translation, Herder and Herder, 1972; originally published in German as *Dialektik der Aufklärung*, Amsterdam: Querido, 1944.

5 Sennett, Richard, *The Fall of Public Man*, New York: Alfred A Knopf, 1976.

6 Kates, Steven, *Twenty Million New Customers: Understanding Gay Men's Consumer Behavior*, Binghamton: Haworth Press, 1998.

Overleaf
Anna Barham, *WHITE CITY*, 2012.
White City Underground station.

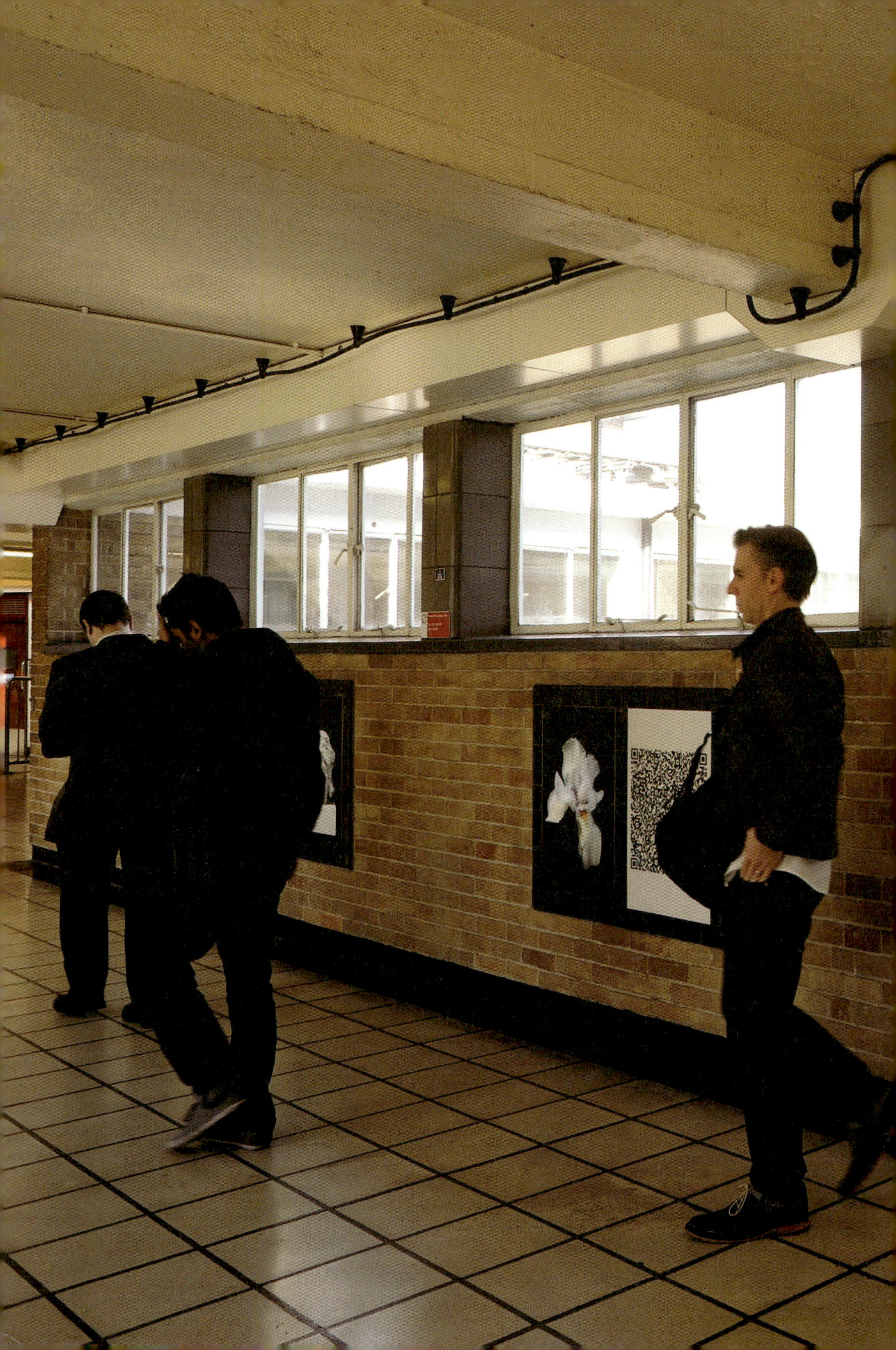

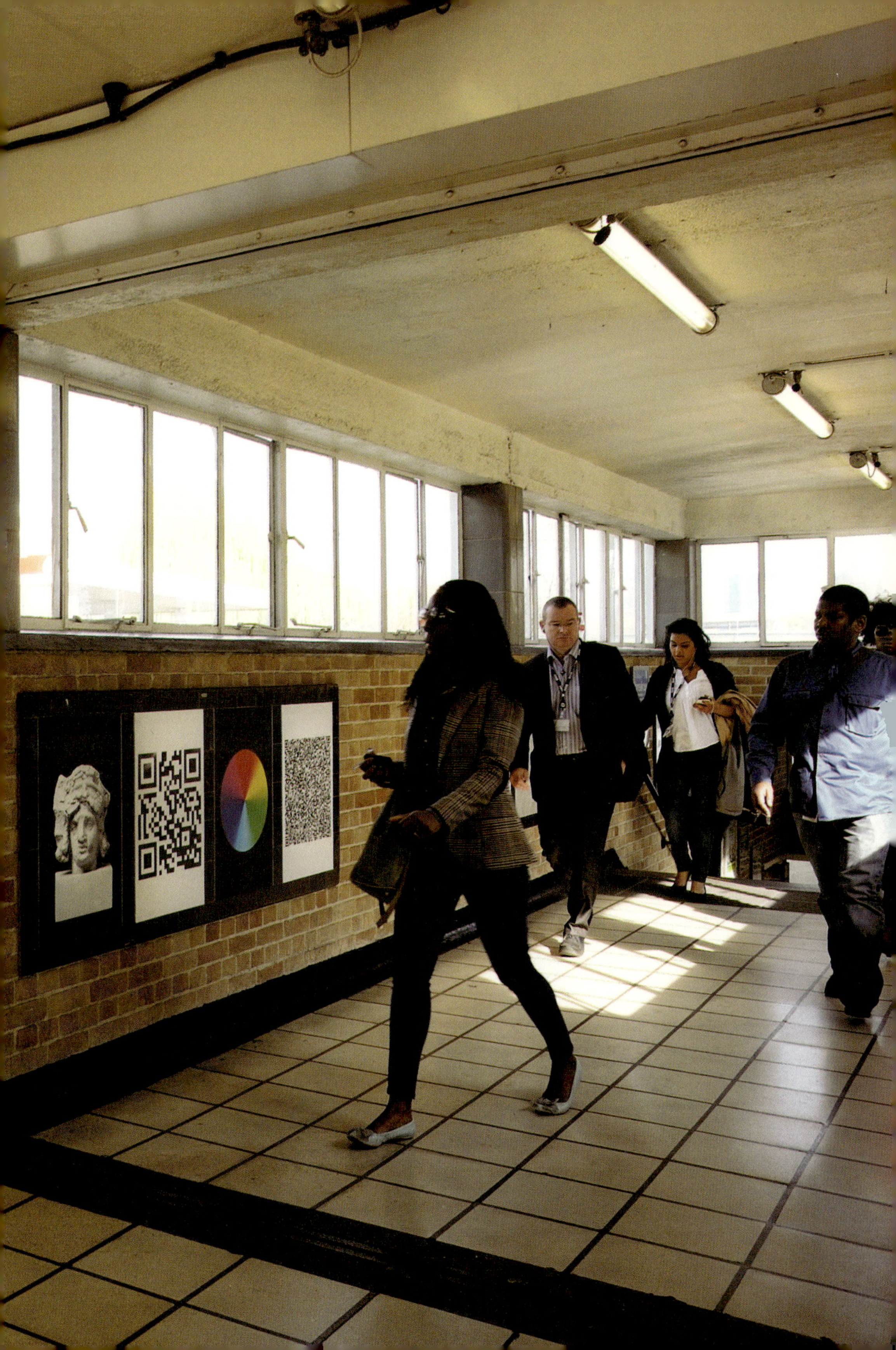

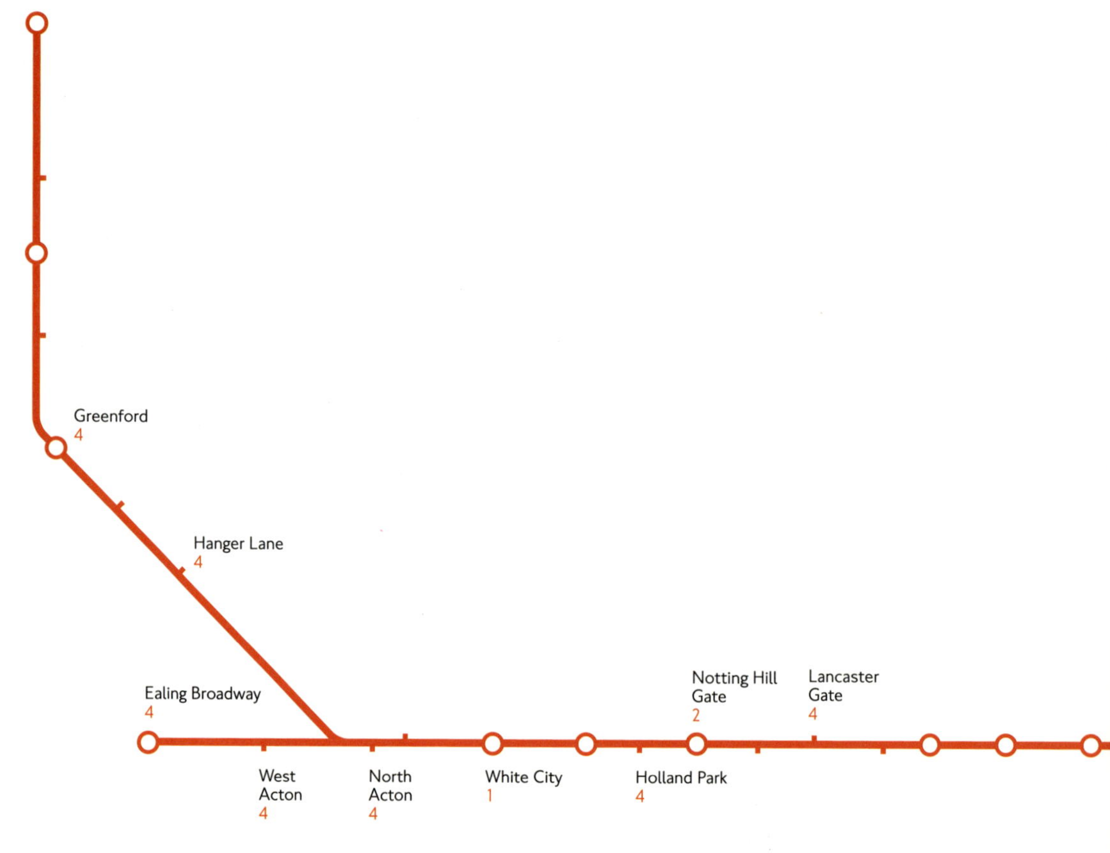

Greenford
4
Hanger Lane
4
Ealing Broadway
4
West
Acton
4
North
Acton
4
White City
1
Holland Park
4
Notting Hill
Gate
2
Lancaster
Gate
4

Projects

In the following pages, each project is represented by information and images, including an artist's biography and photographs of the artworks in-situ, as well as material selected in collaboration with the artists, such as production images and reproductions of archival research. These are intended to enrich understanding of the artists' practices and to reveal the working processes, influences, references and methodologies that they have employed in their approach to the unique context of the Tube.

Artists

1 Anna Barham
WHITE CITY
2 Alice Channer
Hard Metal Body
3 Ruth Ewan
A LOCK IS A GATE
4 Michael Landy
Acts of Kindness
5 Bob and Roberta Smith
and Tim Newton
Who is Community?

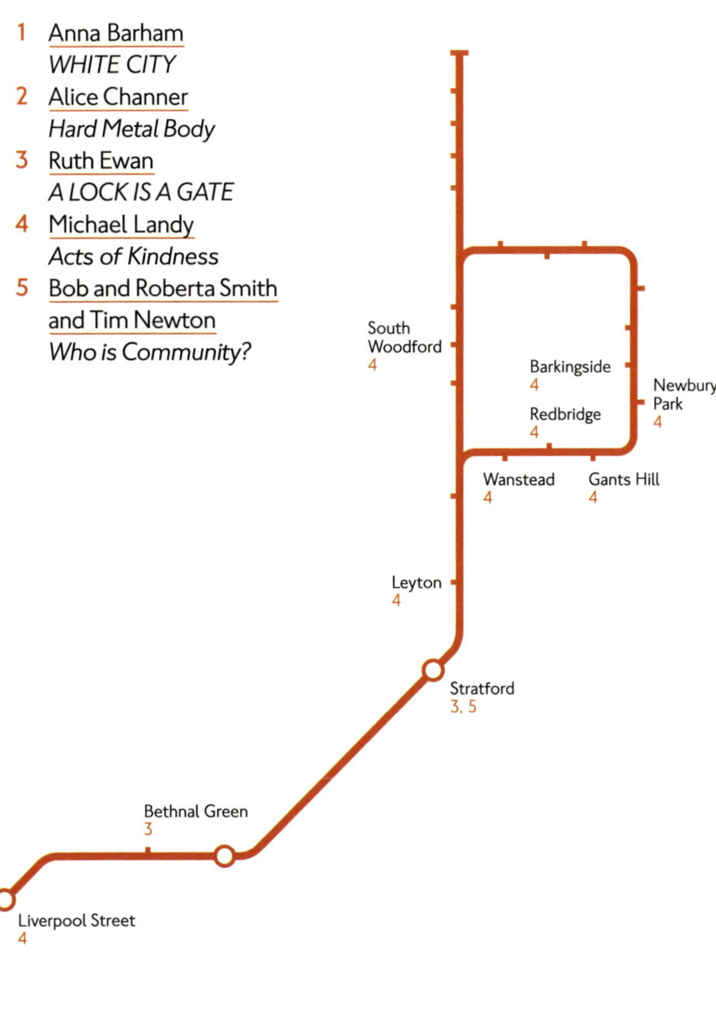

Michael Landy

Acts of Kindness, 2011
Various locations

Michael Landy's practice takes multiple forms, from intimate drawings to ephemeral or short-lived actions. Frequently exploring aspects of consumerism and society, he has made a number of works that involve the wilful destruction of things, possessions and even art. For Art on the Underground, he devised *Acts of Kindness,* a project for which he invited members of the public to share their stories about acts of kindness that they had seen or been a part of on the Tube. As this collection of stories grew online, Landy placed a selection of them in stations and train carriages along the Central line. The project tapped into the zeitgeist of London at the time and garnered a large amount of press coverage (an example of which is included here), which further encouraged people to submit their stories.

The project was a celebration of compassion and generosity, encouraging people to notice acts of kindness, however simple and small. He explains, "Sometimes we tend to assume that you have to be superhuman to be kind, rather than just an ordinary person." To unsettle that idea, *Acts of Kindness* paid attention to those little exchanges that are almost too fleeting and mundane to be noticed or remembered.

Landy first began thinking about the idea behind *Acts of Kindness* immediately after making his work *Break Down* (Artangel, 2001). For *Break Down,* he destroyed all his belongings, from his birth certificate to his car. The experience of being left with nothing helped him reflect on what we are aside from what we own, and on the value of feeling part of a common humanity. "One of the questions that motivated *Break Down*", he says, "was what makes us human, more than just being consumers. I guess I wanted to take that a step further. I was looking for the right situation to explore what value kindness has, what it means, and what kind of exchange is involved in giving someone a helping hand."

The situation he was looking for turned out to be on London Underground. Landy was fascinated by the way in which we tend to disappear into our own bubble on the Tube, disconnected from the people around us. One day, he recalls, while sitting in a Tube train absorbed in his own world, he suddenly became aware of two strangers, one trying to help the other. For Landy it was a life-enhancing event. He wondered what inspires a stranger to be generous to another and created *Acts of Kindness* as a way of capturing and exploring that moment.

Landy defines kindness as going beyond yourself to acknowledge someone else's needs and feelings. "It's a gesture of trust between

Michael Landy, *Acts of Kindness,* 2011.

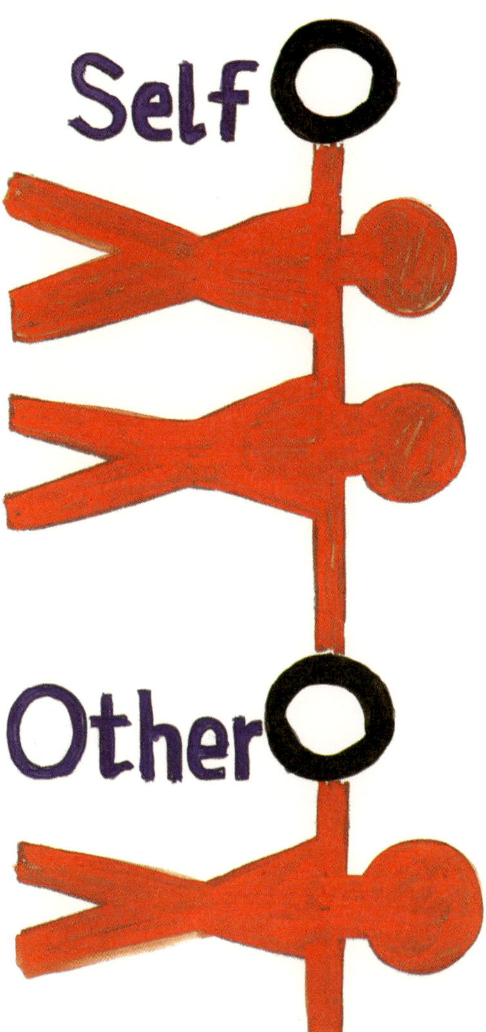

Self
Other
I was trying
to get home from work
in time for my two year old
daughter's bedtime, but had to let
three trains go by as they were too
crowded for me to get on. When the fourth
one came, it was packed with people. I
called into the carriage "please can people
move up, I'm desperate to get home in
time to see my daughter tonight", and
as if by magic, a space opened
up. I got on and strangers
smiled at me.

39

two people", he says. "There's a risk in that. They may just ignore you or take it the wrong way." Acts of kindness between strangers undermine the idea that we should compete and always strive to be independent. Instead, they're an acknowledgement of our shared humanity. "This project is about feeling a sense of being connected to each other", Landy explained. "That's what 'kindness' means— we're kin, we're of one kind."

Michael Landy (born in UK, 1963) was inspired to be an artist when as a child a picture he had made was shown on the BBC TV programme *Take Hart*. After school, he studied art at Loughton, Loughborough and Goldsmiths colleges. Shortly afterwards he achieved acclaim as one of the Young British Artists who transformed the international art scene in the early 1990s. Landy's major projects include *Semi-Detached*, 2004, for which he reproduced his parents' house to scale inside the galleries of Tate Britain, and *Art Bin*, 2010 at the South London Gallery, where he invited artists to come and throw away their work.

Extract from Michael Landy's original proposal

"One of the inspirations for this project came from George Frederic Watts RA 1900 *Memorial To Heroic Self Sacrifice*, located in the Postman's Park in the City of London where ceramic plaques commemorate people who have given their lives to help others, the purpose was to show exemplary behaviour. The choice of texts for *Acts Of Kindness* do not have to be at such heroic levels of sacrifice, but its purpose will be the same and that is to celebrate good selfless deeds by ordinary members of the public that happen on the tube network everyday and go unrecorded."

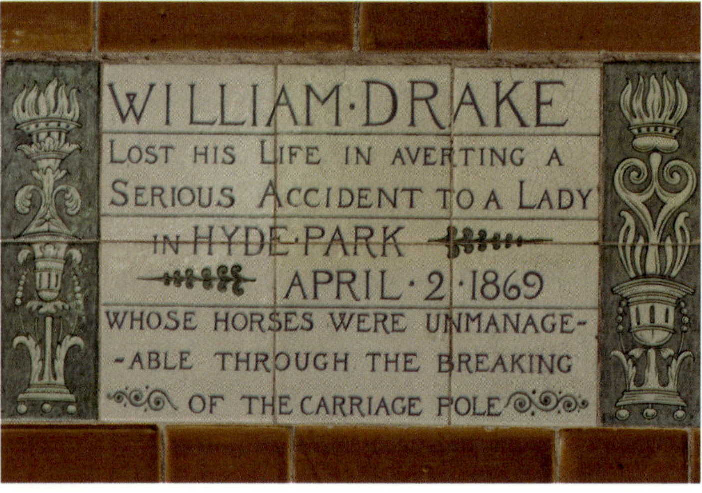

Left
G F Watt, *Memorial to Heroic Self Sacrifice*, Postman's Park, City of London (detail).

Opposite
Acts of Kindness 'call to action' poster, 2011

Overleaf
Michael Landy, *Acts of Kindness*, 2011. Stories installed at 18 Central line stations and train carriages.

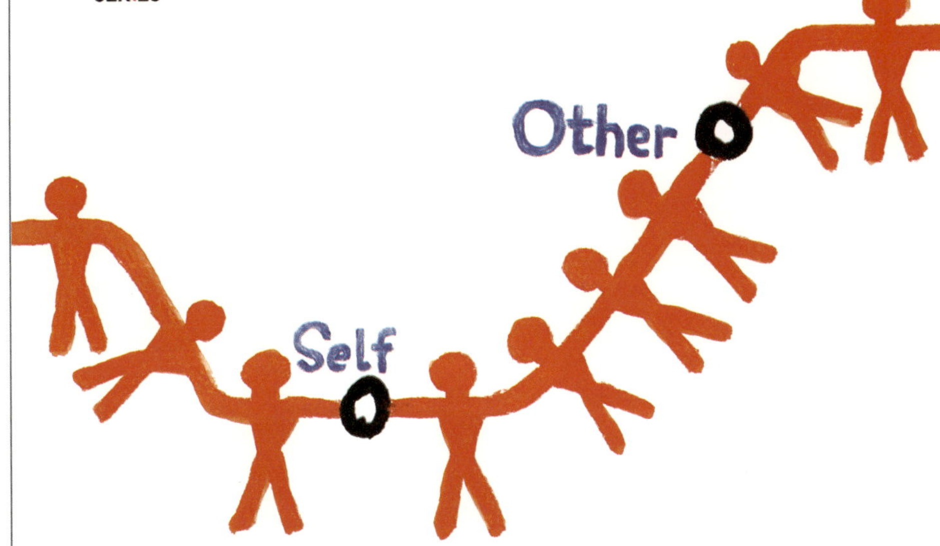

Acts of kindness

Artist Michael Landy wants your stories of kindness on the Tube

Visit art.tfl.gov.uk

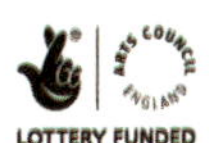

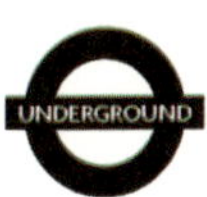

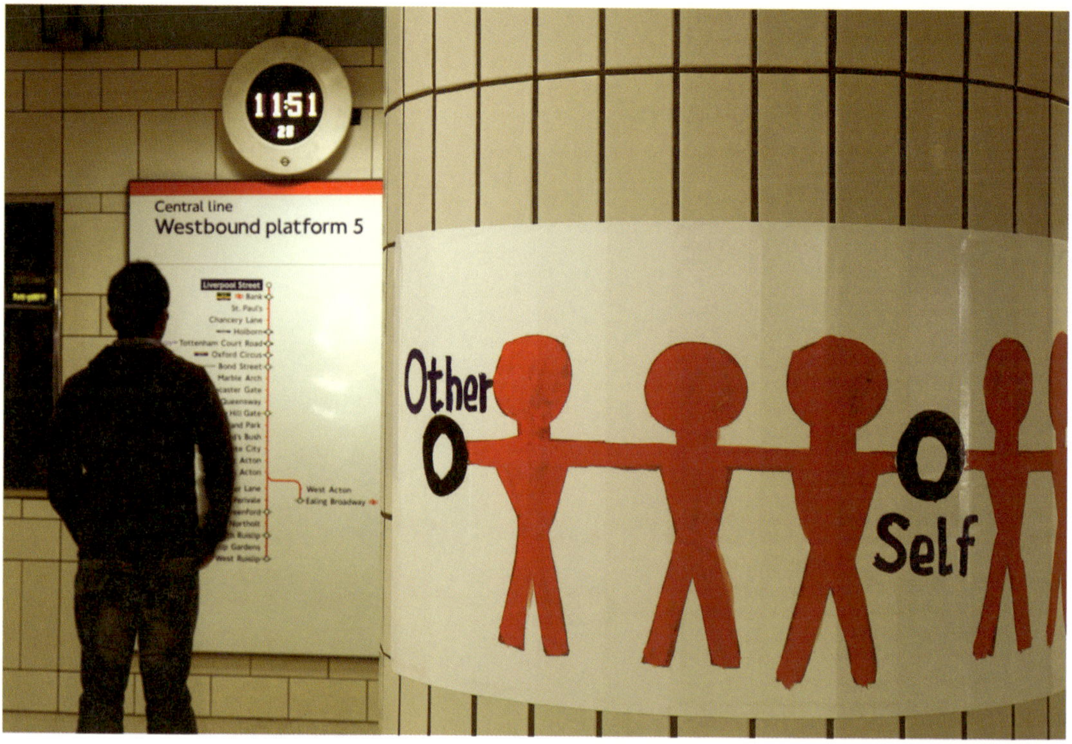

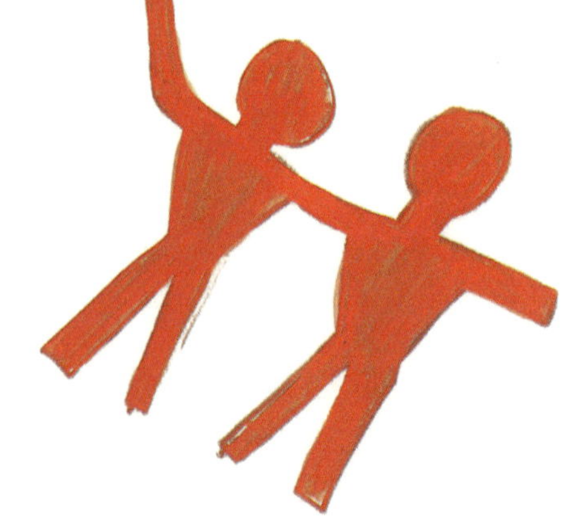

I was trying to
pass an elderly man
in the train to get off. By
coincidence we both kept
stepping in the same direction.
As we eventually got round
each other, he joked, "You
dance divinely." It made me
laugh. It was a sweet
thing to say.

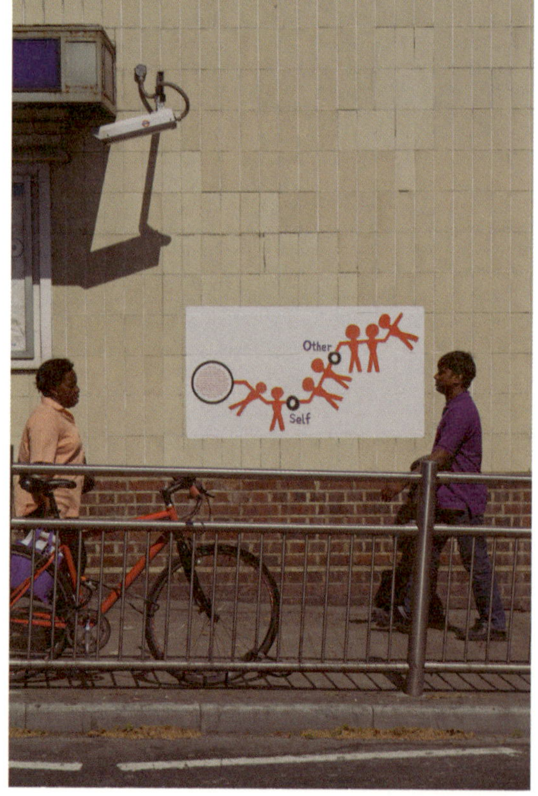

Other
Self

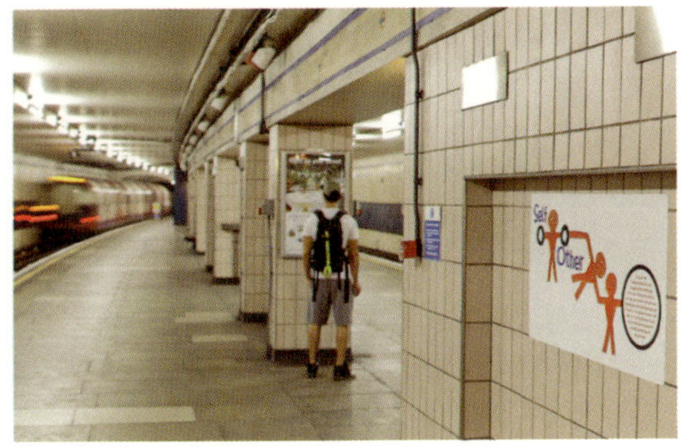

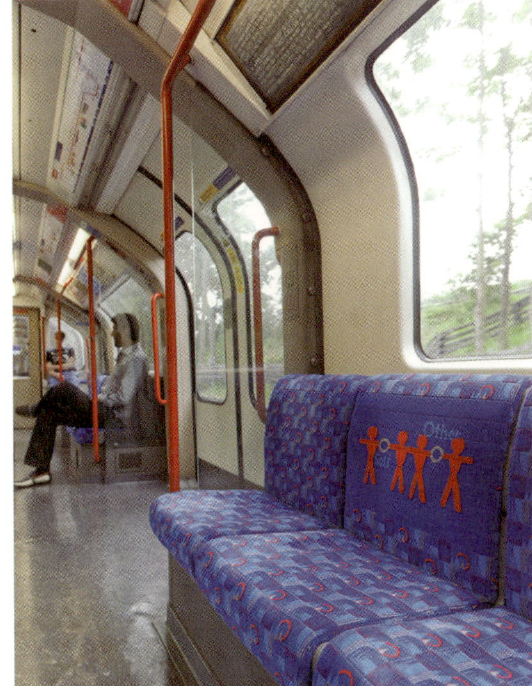

Self
Other

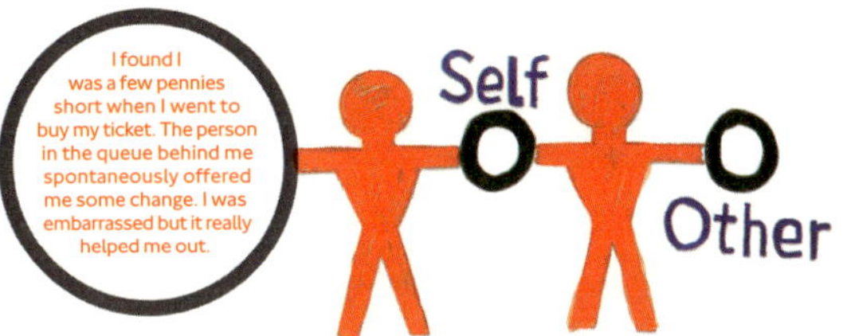

I found I was a few pennies short when I went to buy my ticket. The person in the queue behind me spontaneously offered me some change. I was embarrassed but it really helped me out.

Self
Other

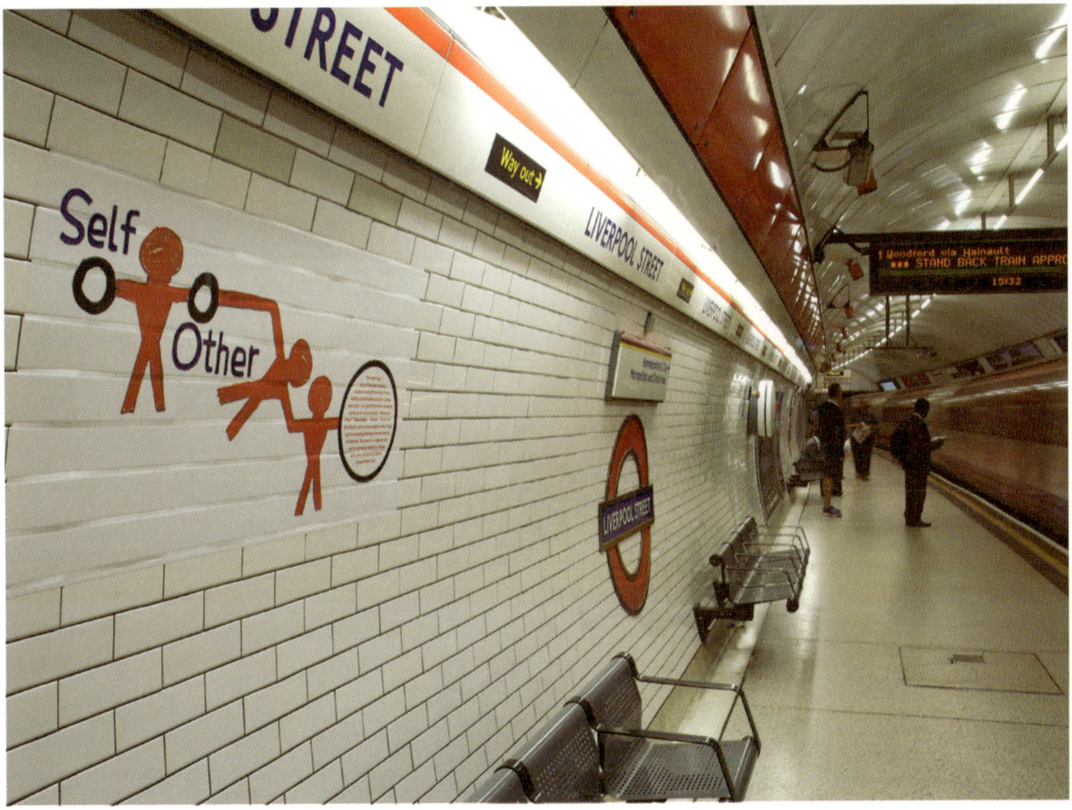

STREET
Way out →
LIVERPOOL STREET
Self
Other
LIVERPOOL STREET
Woodford via Hainault
STAND BACK TRAIN APPRO
15:32

Travelling on the District line one rainy Saturday afternoon, a man sat down next to me and immediately struck up a conversation. Feeling a little wary of this stranger at first, his kind and open nature soon put me at ease. The train was crowded with Chelsea supporters, and when we both got up to leave the carriage he turned to me and said quietly, "The quality of your life is determined by the quality of your thoughts." Those words felt so profound then, and they still do. I have the quote on a piece of paper that sits next to my computer at work. I read it every day and it reminds me that we can learn so much from the people around us—even complete strangers.

One morning on the Jubilee line a woman lent over and removed a small amount of shaving foam I'd somehow left on my ear. On an over-crowded train to Canary Wharf, it made me and the person next to me smile. Literally, a touching act of kindness (or mercy?)

I stopped to help a collapsed man who was obviously in extremis, and I thought at first, having a fit. It became clear that he was having the most severe form of asthma attack (*status asthmaticus*) and was at risk of dying. Another doctor and I called for help and checked over the man, but we had no equipment or drugs on us (neither of us was working). Then, a train stopped and I shouted to ask if anyone had an inhaler. After passing through two or three carriages, a mother handed over her small son's inhaler. Seeing the man on the platform through the windows she paused, and, I imagine, pictured her son in that state, then handed over her boy's 'spacer' complete with cherished child's stickers. The doors closed as she bent down to explain to the alarmed toddler why his 'puffer' had just been given to an alarming shouting strange man and I raced back to the collapsed man. Her quick thinking and generosity with her son's spacer saved the man's life, as he was too far gone to use an inhaler without it. I never got to thank her, nor find out if she realised quite how important her quick thinking and kindness were.

A selection of stories chosen by Michael Landy for this publication.

Right
A media campaign from summer 2011, including posters displayed on the Underground, encouraged the public to submit their own 'acts of kindness'.

Overleaf
Working drawings and ideas for *Acts of Kindness*.

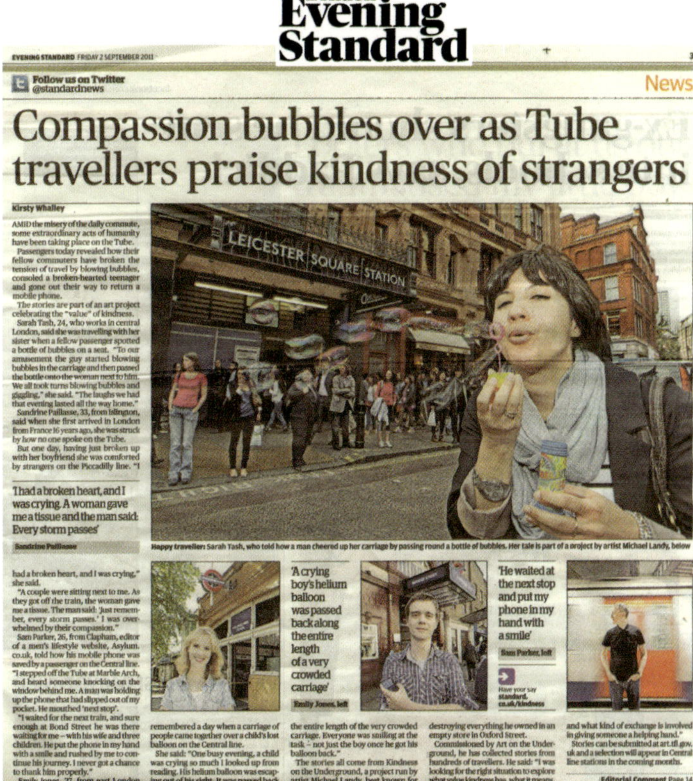

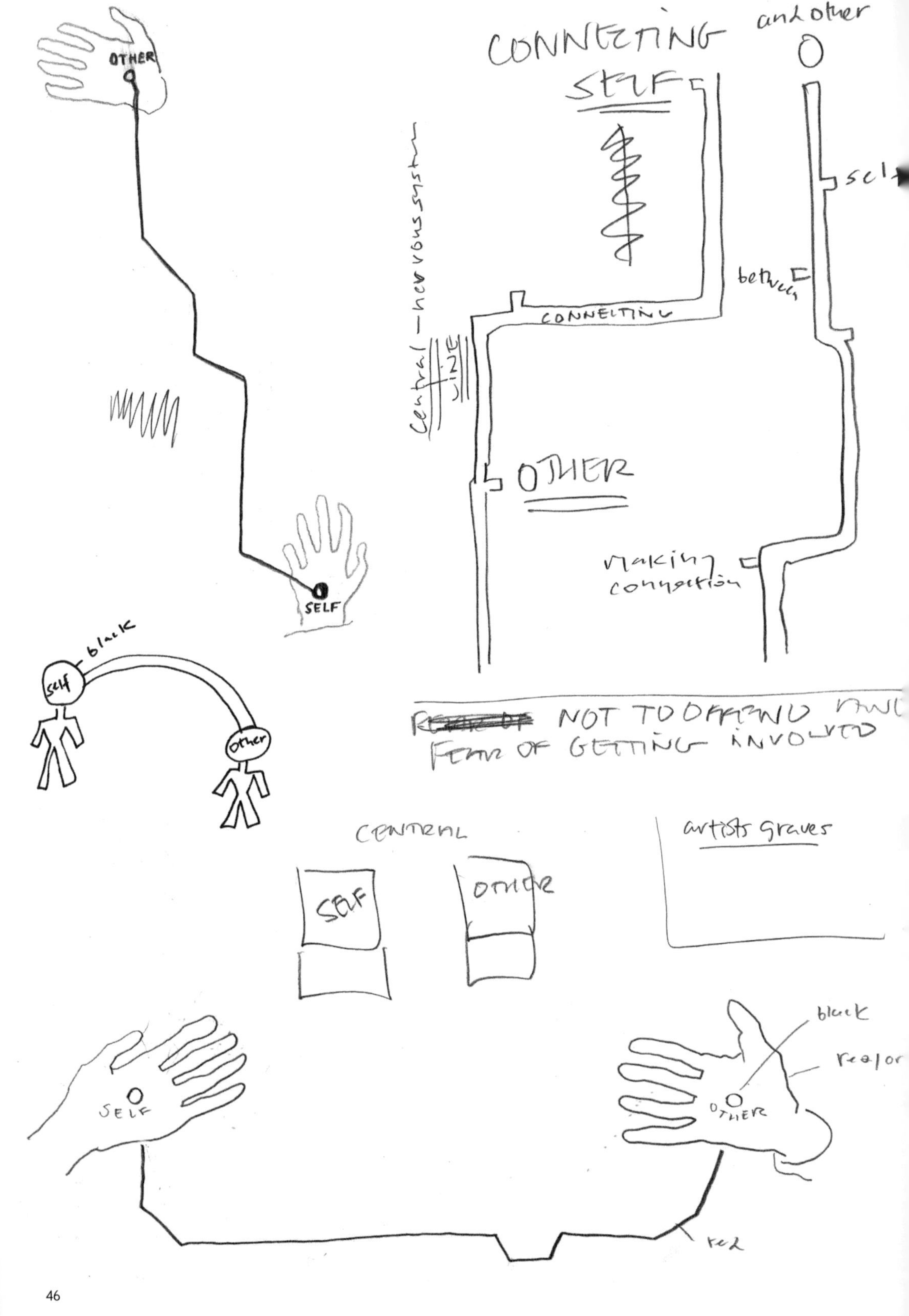

OTHER
SELF
CONNECTING and other
SELF
Central — nervous system
LINE
CONNECTING
between
sel
OTHER
making connection
black
Self
Other
NOT TO OFFEND and
FEAR OF GETTING INVOLVED
CENTRAL
SELF
OTHER
artists graves
SELF
black
real or
OTHER
real
46

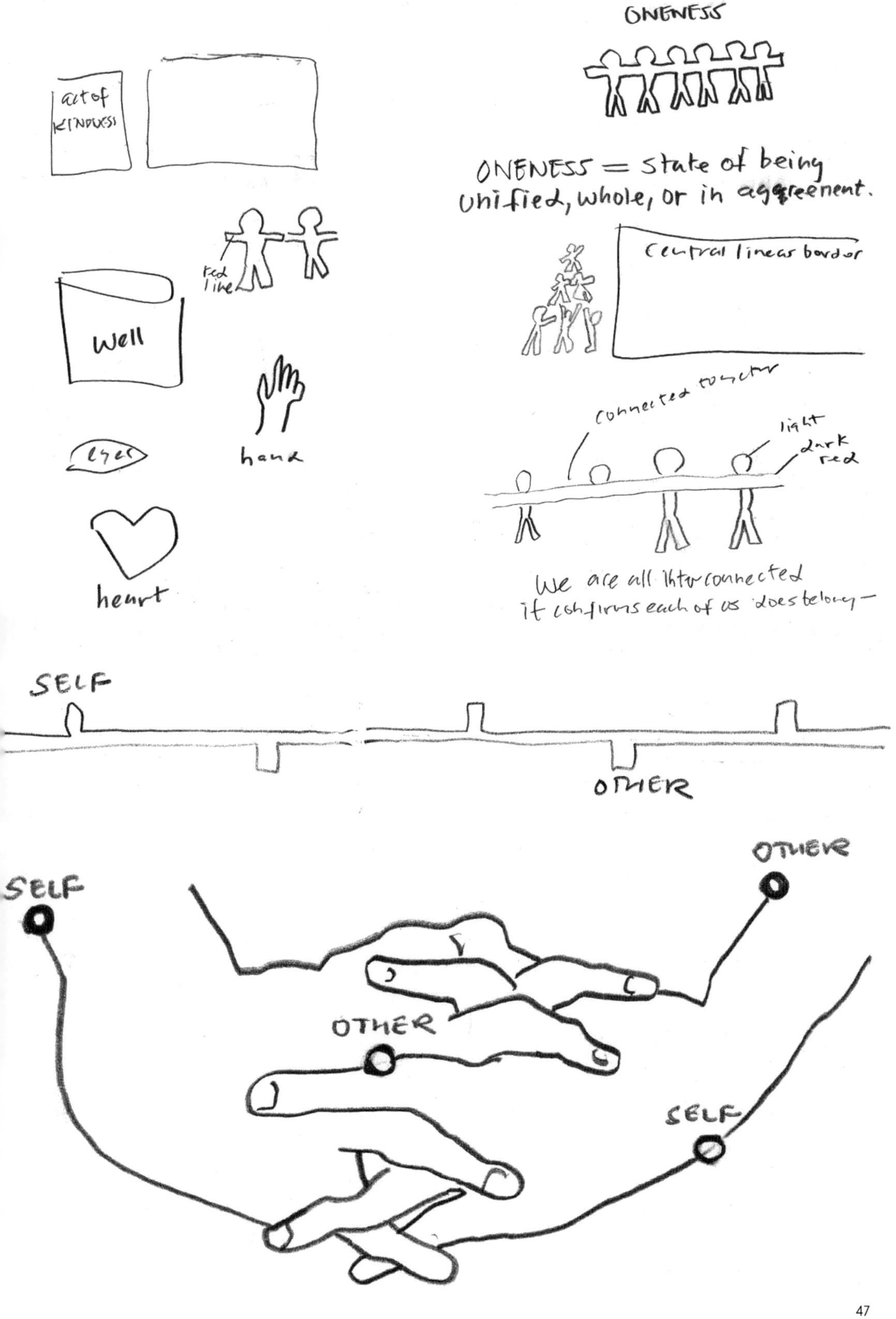

ONENESS = state of being
unified, whole, or in agreement.

We are all interconnected
it confirms each of us does belong —

Ruth Ewan

A LOCK IS A GATE, 2011
Bethnal Green and Stratford Underground stations

Ruth Ewan's practice explores links between culture and music as a means of personal expression. Often summoning the forgotten histories of grassroots movements, she foregrounds moments from the past in the present. Finding resonance with the ethos of folk music, she suggests that listening and looking can be a means of coming together and enacting change. *A LOCK IS A GATE* evolved from an initial idea by Ewan to create an album with a group of young people using only their voices and sounds.

Ewan invited composer Kerry Andrew and poet Evlynn Sharp to collaborate on *A LOCK IS A GATE*. The project involved young people from the Laburnum Boat Club youth project in Hackney. Nearly 40 members of the Club aged nine to 19 years old took part in creating an album of experimental songs, a book of drawings, posters for the Tube network and artworks for Bethnal Green and, later, Stratford Underground stations. All the voices, words and drawings from the project were the participants' own.

A LOCK IS A GATE weaved sounds, songs and drawings into a part-real, part-imagined journey that wound across London from the Tube to the canal. Along the way the young voyagers passed through an extensive canal tunnel and negotiated a lock. A lock on a canal is a water-gate that lets a boat pass through different levels of water. In the title song, the lock stands both for a real canal lock and for the obstacles that we all face in life.

A special edition of the album as a CD was created with sleeve artwork and a book of drawings that took a journey in parallel with the songs. The drawings and texts evolved from the young people's experiences and reflections collected during the project. The CD was available from Bethnal Green station and the nearby V&A Museum of Childhood. In addition, the album was accessible from the Art on the Underground website.

Two artworks were developed to run the length of the escalators at Bethnal Green station. These were based on drawings created in response to two of the album songs.

A LOCK IS A GATE was selected from a series of invited artists' proposals for commission by Art on the Underground in partnership with the Barbican Art Gallery, Chisenhale Gallery, Create Festival and the Whitechapel Gallery.

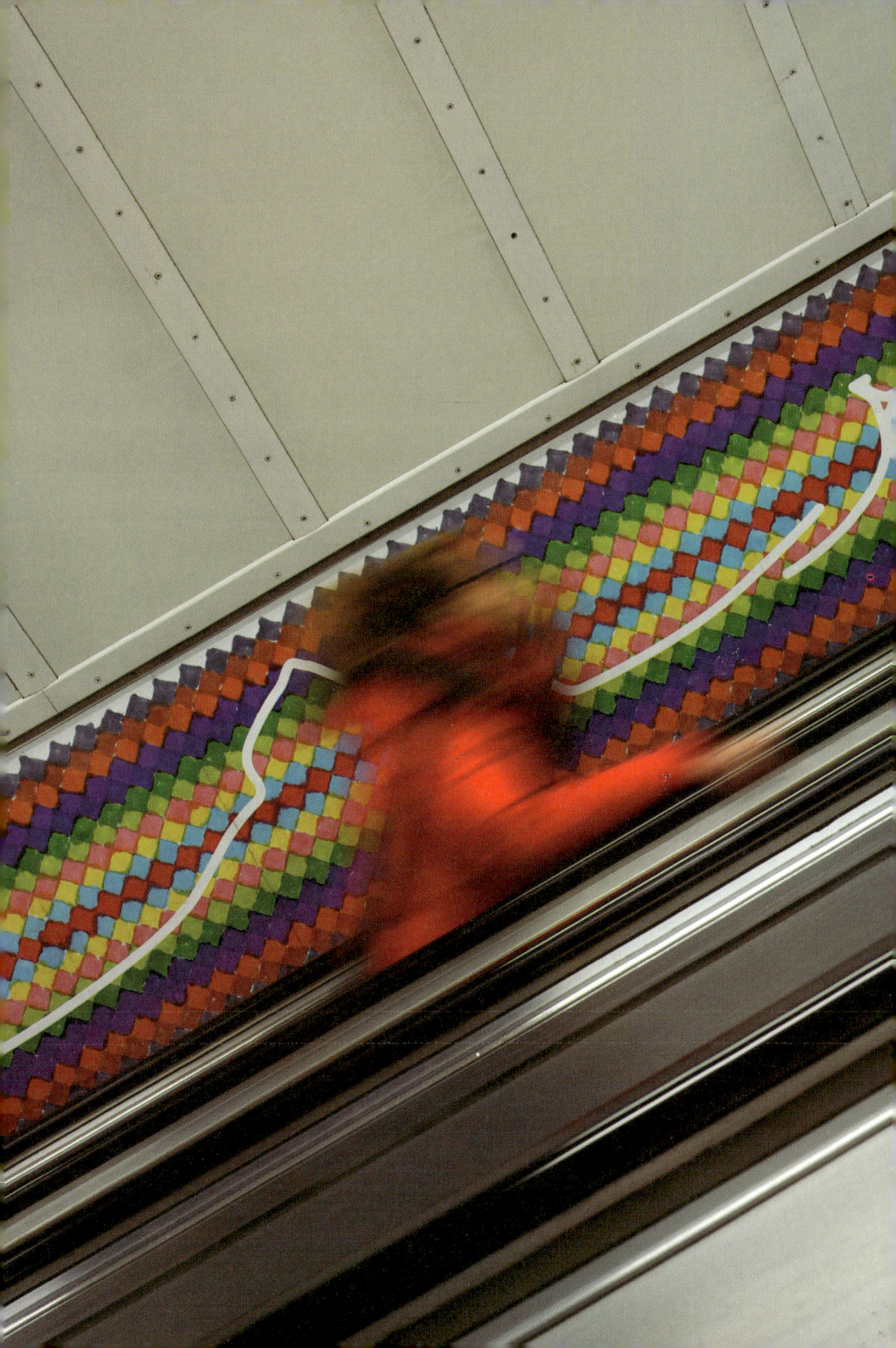

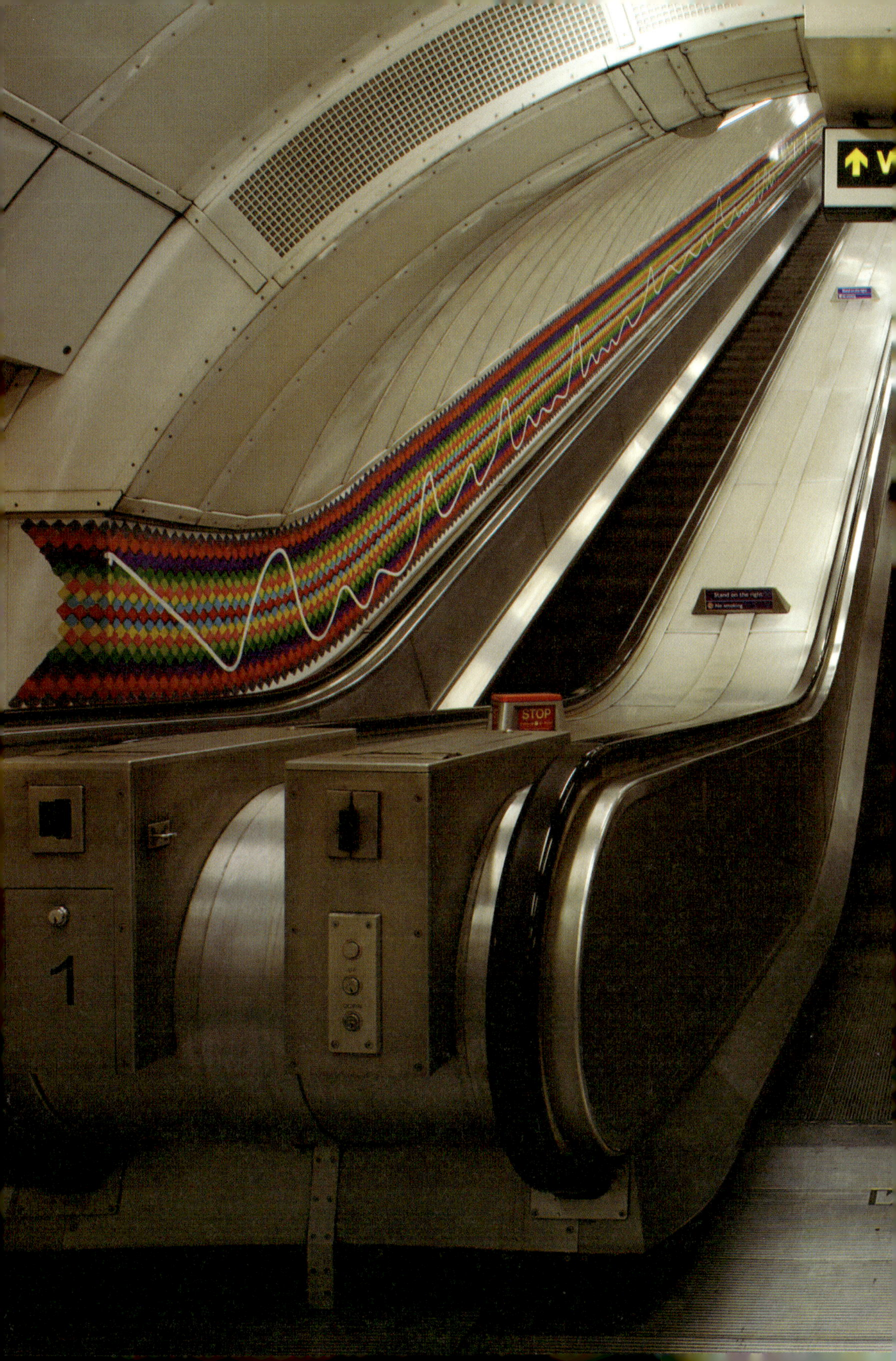

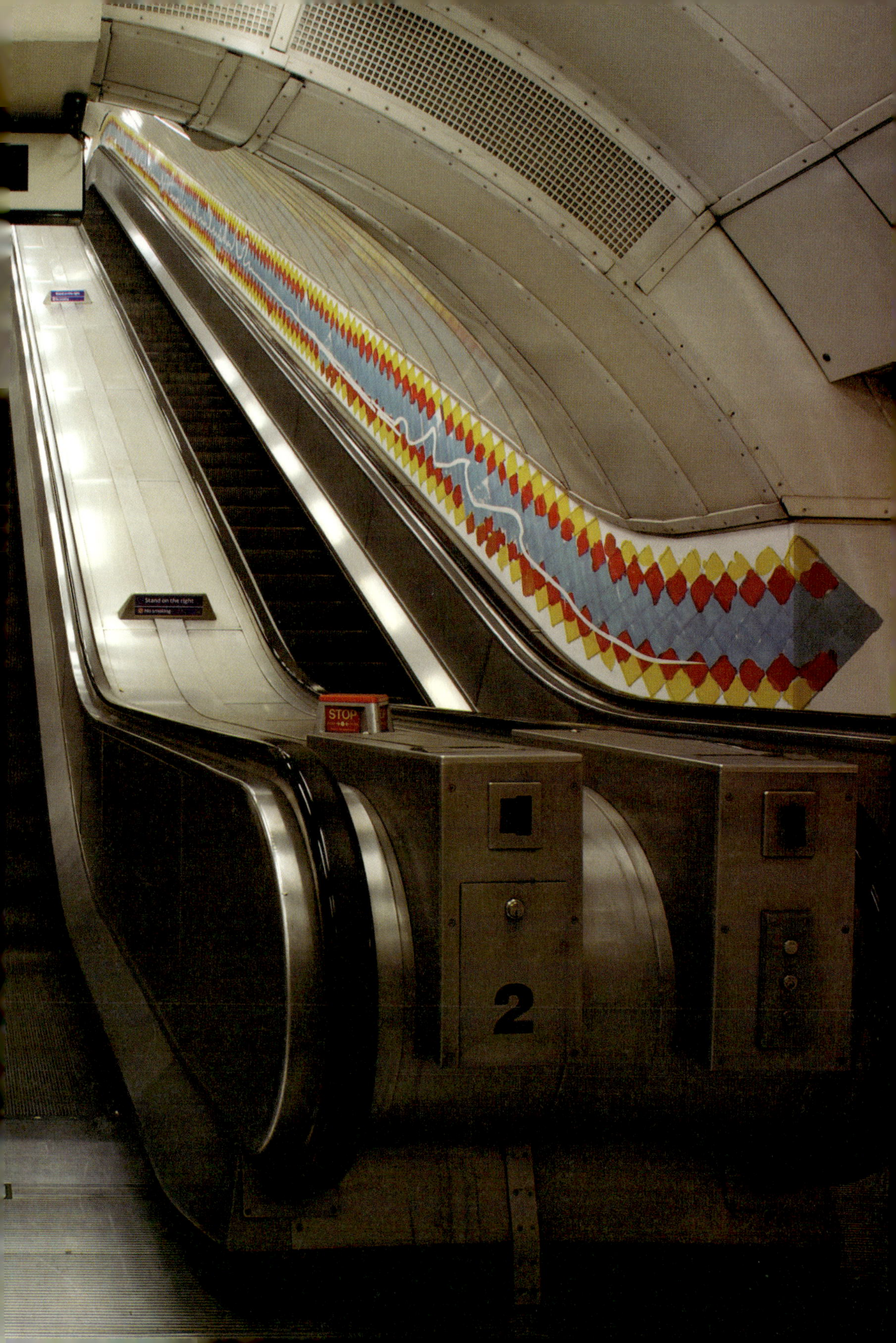

Stand on the right
No smoking
STOP
2

Ruth Ewan (born in Scotland, 1980) studied at the Edinburgh
College of Art, and is based in London. Recent solo shows and
projects include *Brank & Heckle*, Dundee Contemporary Arts,
UK, 2011; *Liberties of The Savoy*, Frieze Projects London, UK,
2012; *Music Without Masters*, Badischer Kunstverein, Karlsruhe,
Germany, 2012. The artist's recent group exhibitions include
The Human Pattern, Kunsthall Oslo, Norway, 2011; *Younger Than
Jesus*, New Museum, New York, USA, 2009; *Altermodern: Tate
Triennial*, Tate Britain, London, UK, 2009; *Life*, Louisiana Museum
of Modern Art, Humlebæk, Denmark, 2011.

Kerry Andrew is a composer, performer, writer and educator whose
works have been broadcast on both BBC 6Music and BBC Radio 3.

Evlynn Sharp is an award-winning poet, playwright and educator.

Laburnum Boat Club in Hackney is a social-education facility
concerned with the development of children and young people
of all abilities, primarily through watersport activities.

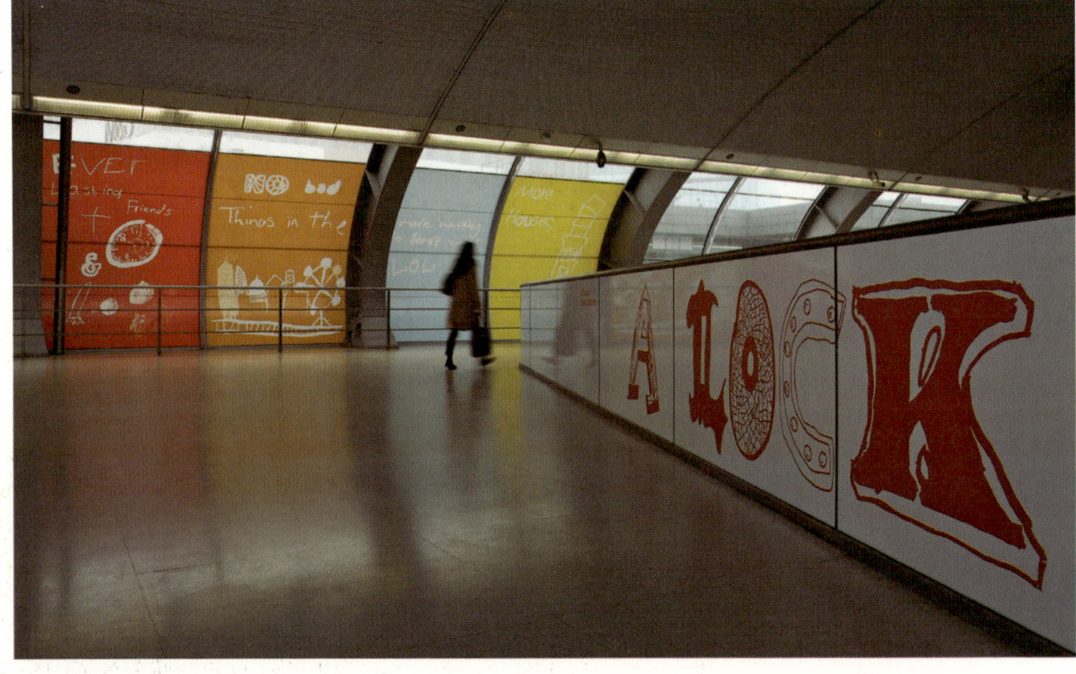

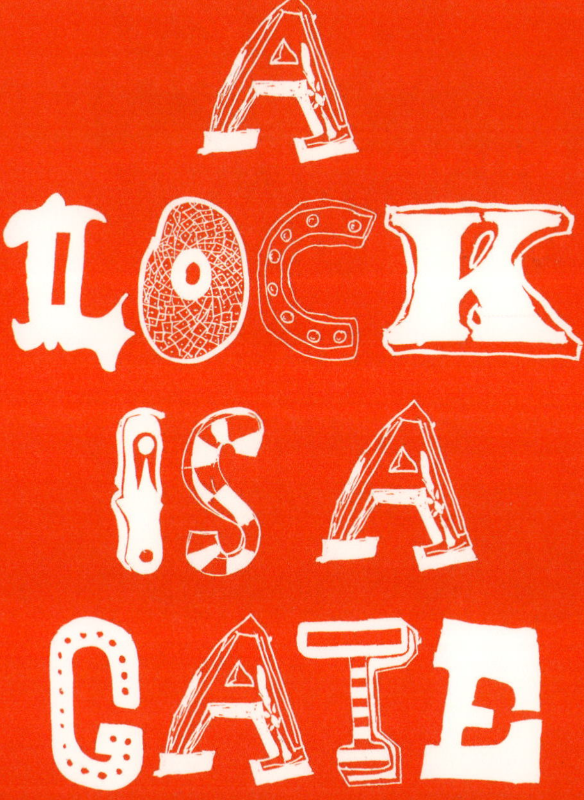

ART ON THE UNDERGROUND
CENTRAL LINE SERIES

A LOCK IS A GATE

A mini concept album and drawing project
devised by artist Ruth Ewan with composer
Kerry Andrew and poet Evlynn Sharp and created by
members of the Laburnum Boat Club in Hackney

Download the album tracks and find out
about the project at art.tfl.gov.uk

Image copyright © Ruth Ewan 2011. Poster design by Rose.

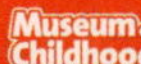
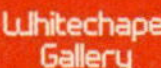

Laburnum BOAT CLUB
barbican
CHISENHALE GALLERY
Create
Museum of Childhood
Whitechapel Gallery

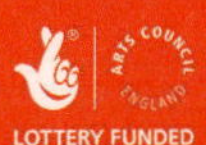

ARTS COUNCIL ENGLAND
LOTTERY FUNDED

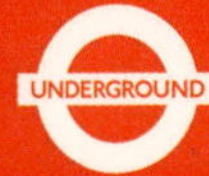

UNDERGROUND

MAYOR OF LONDON
Transport for London

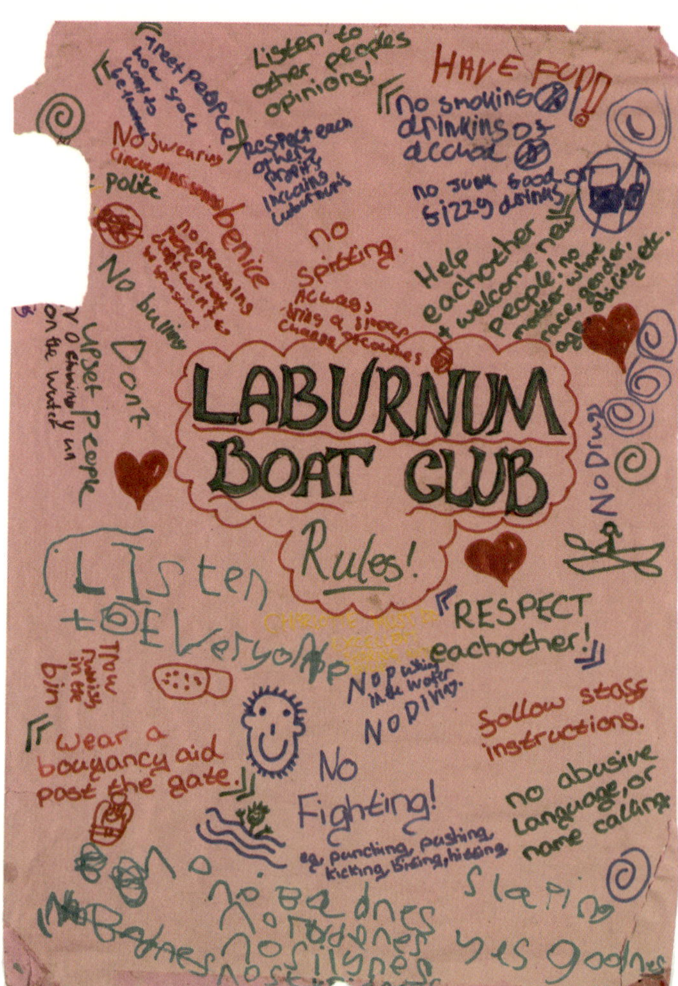

Left
Laburnum Boat Club Rules,
summer 2011. Every six months
the members of the Club add new
rules. The Laburnum Boat Club
Rules are a work-in-progress, that
way everyone at the Club takes
part in making them. The Rules
were made into a poster insert in
the album sleeve for *A LOCK IS
A GATE*.

Below and Opposite
Canal boat journey and workshops.
Drawings and song lyrics by
Laburnum Boat Club members.

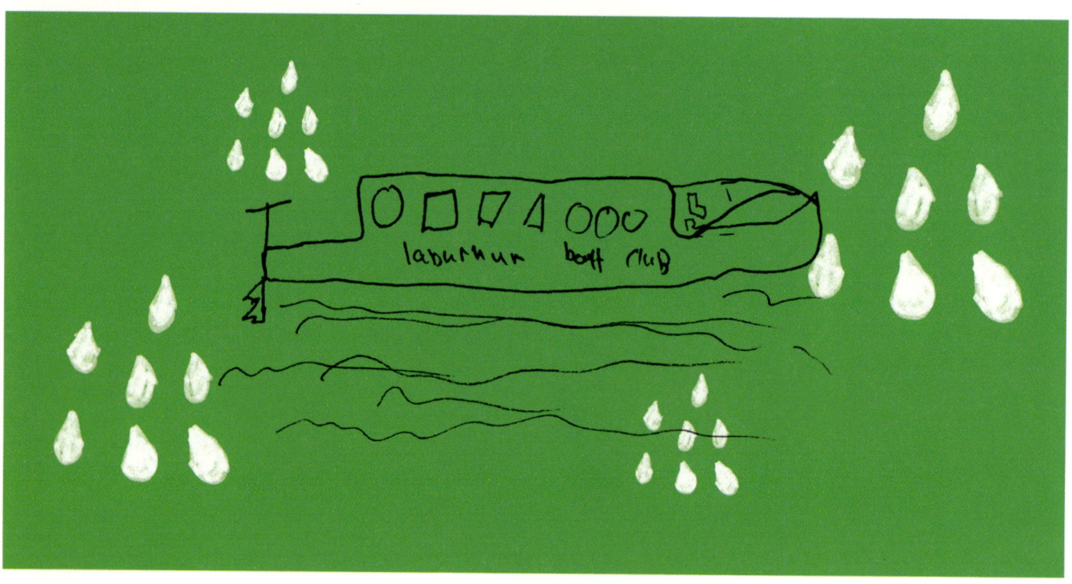

Live forever machine
Equal Money Machine
Water machine
Food Machine

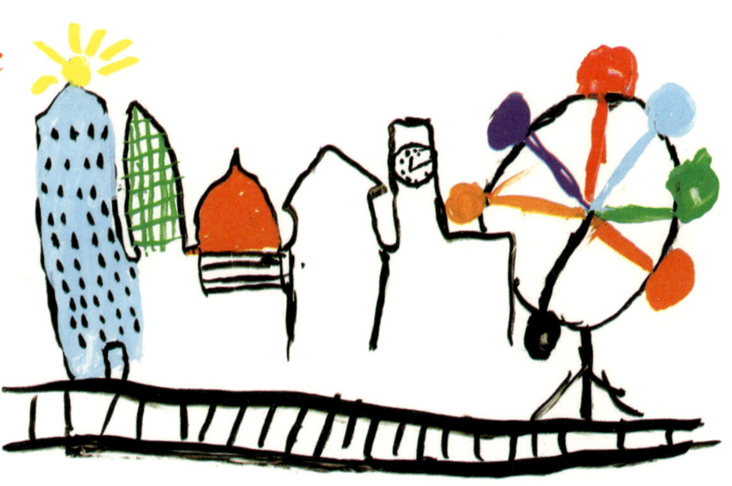

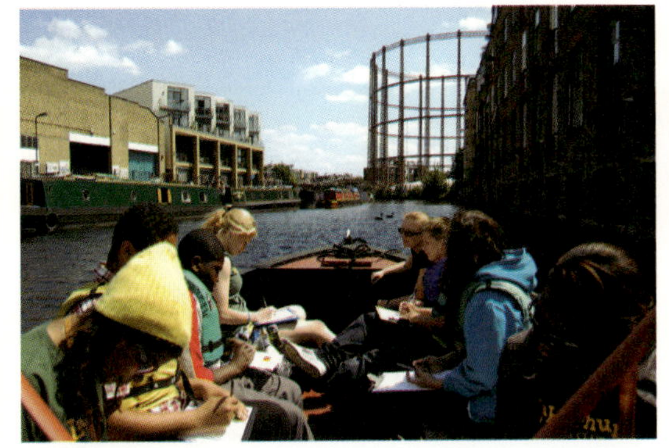

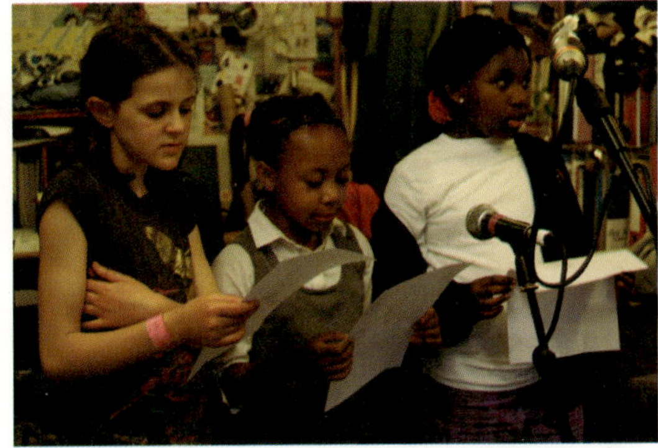

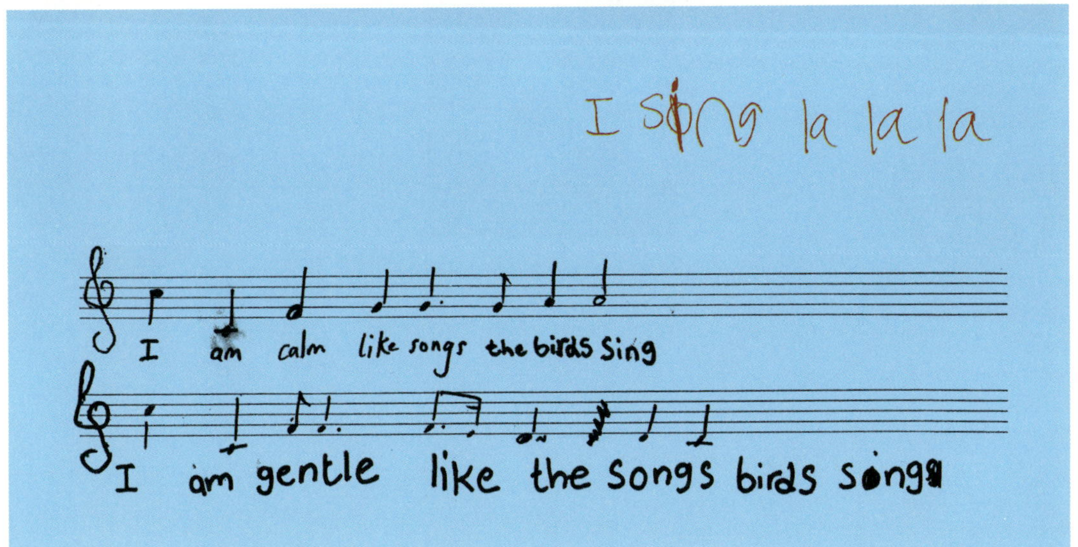

LADY MILDMAY
COMMUNITY NARROWBOAT
LABURNUM BOAT CLUB

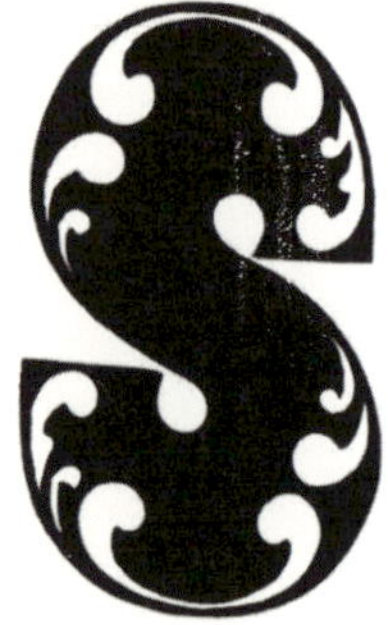 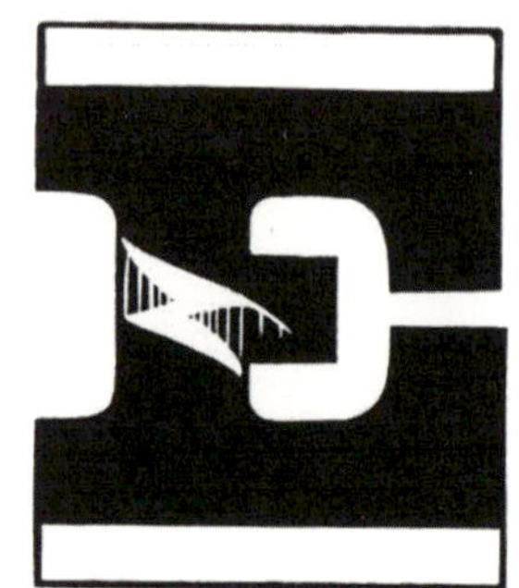 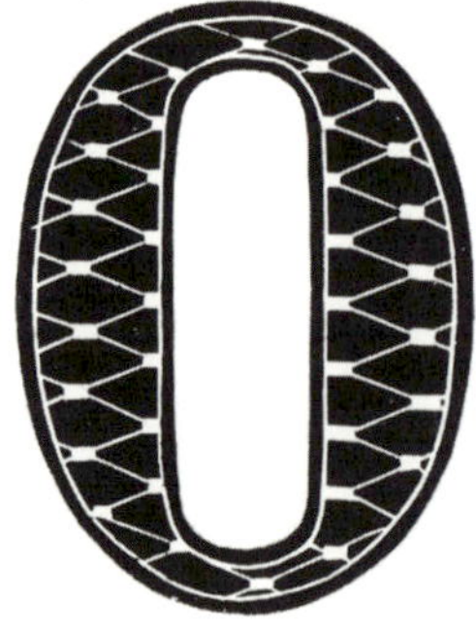

Opposite, top
A lock and tunnel on the Regent's Canal
as seen from a canal boat.

Above
Barge lettering that inspired
the group to produce their
own typography.

Opposite, bottom
London Transport leaflets c 1947,48 when
the Central line was extended eastwards.

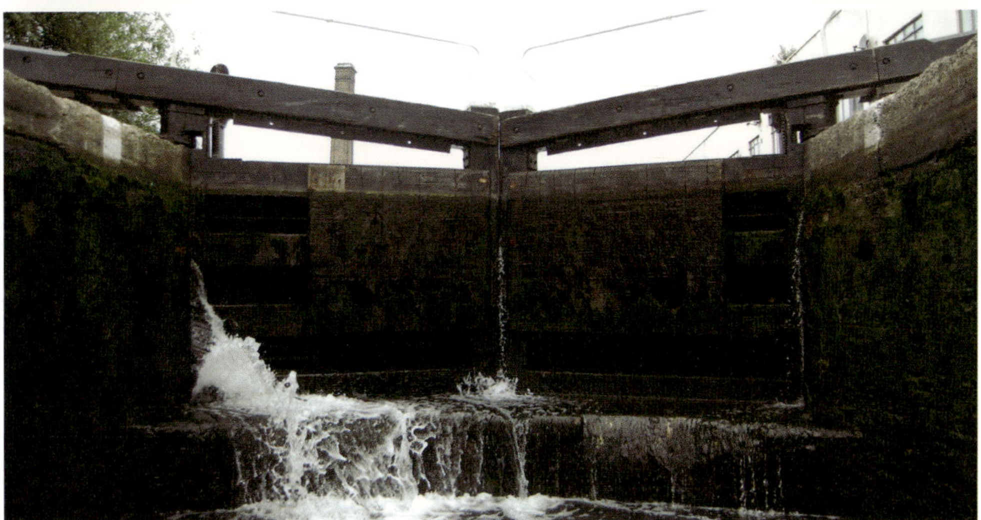

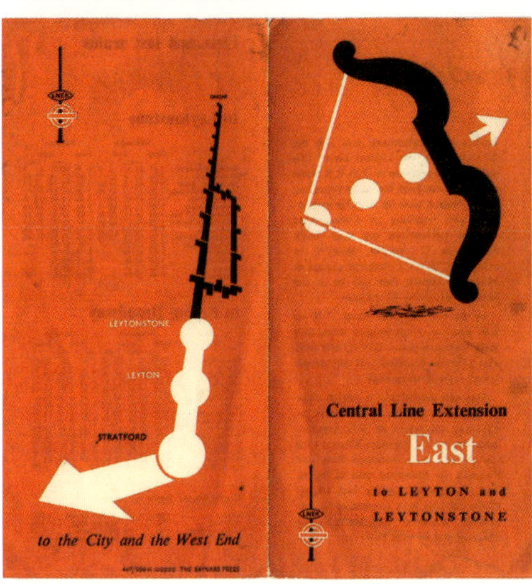
LEYTONSTONE
LEYTON
STRATFORD
to the City and the West End
Central Line Extension
East
to LEYTON and
LEYTONSTONE

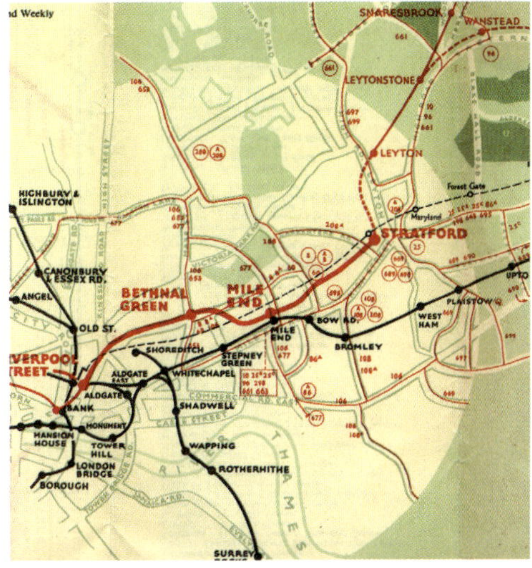
nd Weekly
SNARESBROOK
WANSTEAD
LEYTONSTONE
LEYTON
Forest Gate
HIGHBURY &
ISLINGTON
Maryland
STRATFORD
CANONBURY
ESSEX RD.
BETHNAL
GREEN
MILE
END
Angel
PLAISTOW
OLD ST.
BOW RD.
WEST
HAM
SHOREDITCH
STEPNEY
GREEN
BROMLEY
LIVERPOOL
STREET
ALDGATE
EAST
WHITECHAPEL
MILE
END
BANK
ALDGATE
SHADWELL
MANSION
HOUSE
MONUMENT
WAPPING
TOWER
HILL
LONDON
BRIDGE
ROTHERHITHE
BOROUGH
THAMES
SURREY

Anna Barham

WHITE CITY, 2012
White City Underground station

Anna Barham's works are informed by her longstanding interest in the processes of constructing meaning through language. She often explores the malleable nature of language by using text like building material that can be reconfigured into new combinations.

WHITE CITY was a project in two parts: a series of posters at the station and a group of directly related video and text works to be viewed using a smartphone. The multiple elements that constituted the work drew on the architecture and history of the station as well as the journeys that the artist made along the Central line.

In this work, Barham exploited the functional aspect and form of QR codes and incorporated them into the series of posters. As a commonplace symbol, a QR code has no meaning of its own. It is defined by its function as a graphic-data storage device and requires a smartphone application to decode the information it carries. Rather than the solid colour that usually makes up the codes, Barham used their pixellated form to cut through photographic images, 'corrupting' and fragmenting them. Taken during journeys that Barham made along the Central line, the images reflect her fascination with the interiors of empty stations and train carriages, the design of the upholstery, and Eduardo Paolozzi's mosaics at Tottenham Court Road Underground station.

An important feature of the project was the fact that the series of 'portable' text and video works accessed through the QR code posters would be viewed on a phone screen. This gave a jewel-like quality to the videos and an intimate, one-to-one aspect for viewing them. The use of the QR codes also reflects the increasing use of smartphones to watch movies and video clips online.

In previous works, Barham's investigations into the flexible and imprecise nature of language have led her to use combinatory methods such as anagrams to disclose hidden meanings. In this work, from the letters of White City emerged the word "Tyche", the Greek goddess of chance and fortune, who became the main figure for one of the videos and a presiding metaphor for the project.

Also based on the play of letters are the other two videos embedded in the posters, each presenting animations of anagrams of station names along the Central Line. (East Acton becomes EAST CANTO, A CANTO SET, ACT ON A SET, CAT ON A SET and so on). Another set of QR posters links the viewer to a quote by the philosopher Ludwig Wittgenstein that helps contextualise Barham's approach to language (see quote 3 on p.65).

Anna Barham, *Eastbound*,
video still, 2012.

WHITE CITY
WE HIT CITY
CY WET HIT
CE THY WIT
I WIT TYCHE

USH BE SPED SHH

Viewers were left to assemble and reassemble the multiple elements that made *WHITE CITY* in order to make their own 'route' through the work, and draw their own conclusions. Barham's exploration and manipulation of the QR codes was a new development in her practice, using technology in an innovative way to pursue her long-lasting exploration into the plurality of ways in which we make sense of the world through language.

Anna Barham (born in UK, 1974) currently lives and works in London. She graduated from the Slade School of Fine Art, London, in 2001. Barham has exhibited internationally and within the UK. Recent solo exhibitions include *Warp and Woof* (with Bea McMahon), CCA Glasgow, UK, 2011; *A Splintered Game*, Galerie Nordenhake, Stockholm, Sweden, 2011 and *Anna Barham*, International Project Space, Birmingham, UK, 2010. Group exhibitions include *Formes Breves*, Autres, 25, FRAC Lorraine, Metz, France, 2012; *Graphology*, The Drawing Room, London, UK, 2012; *Provisional Information, Occasionals*, MK Gallery, Milton Keynes, UK, 2011; *Graphology Chapter 3*, MHKA, Antwerp, Belgium, 2011; *Poor.Old.Tired.Horse*, ICA, London, UK, 2009 and *Stutter*, Tate Modern, London, UK, 2009.

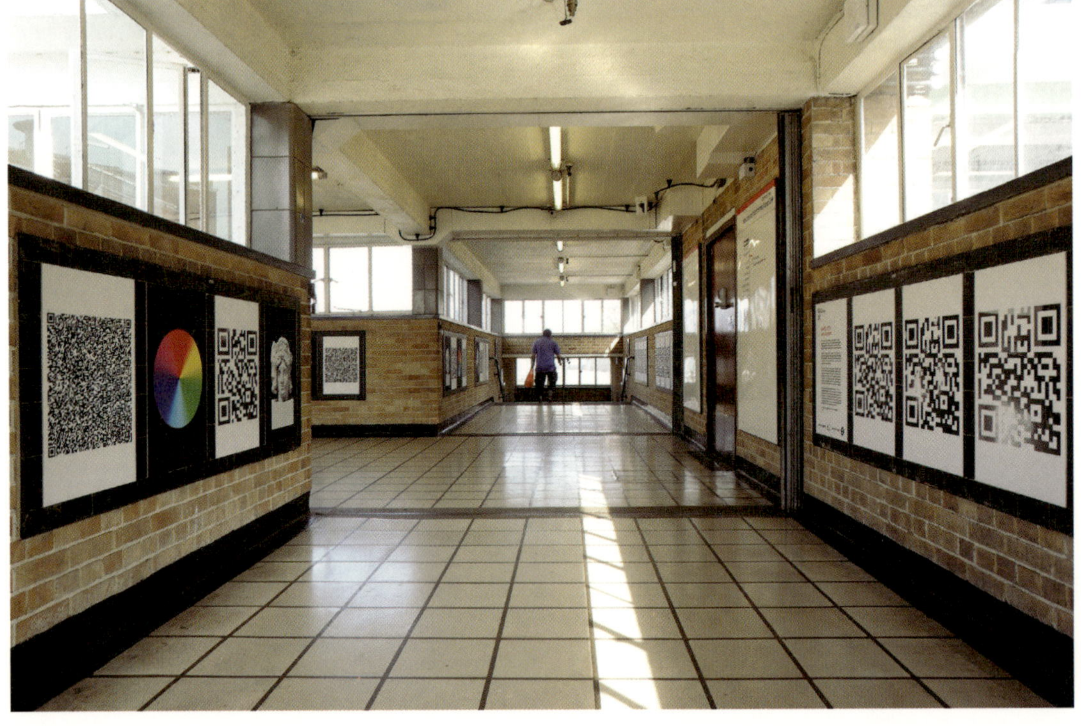

LIVERPOOL STREET
LOVELIER PROTEST
LOVELIEST REPORT
TOILER OVERSLEPT
TO PLOT REVELRIES
STEELIER VOLT PRO
RELIEVES PLOT ROT
OR OVERSLEEP TILT
TROT OVER ELLIPSE
TROT LOVE REPLIES
TO REPTILE LOVERS
RESTIVE PLOT ROLE
RESPELL VOTE RIOT
RETELL SORE PIVOT
RETELL OVER POSIT
REPELS VIOLET ROT
OVER SPOTLIT REEL
RIVE LETTER LOOPS
LIVE LETTER SPOOR
OR TILT SLEEPOVER
LIP TOOT REVELERS
TO SPOILT REVELER
LILT TOO PERVERSE
TILL TOO PERVERSE
REVERSE TILT LOOP
REVERSE LIP LOTTO
REVERSE POOL TILT
OVERT PLOT RELIES
PERT SERVILE TOOL
LET SERVILE TROOP
TELLS TO OVERRIPE
OR TELL POVERTIES
TO SPELL OVERTIRE
LO PRETTIER LOVES
LO PETTIER LOVERS
RETIE LOVERS PLOT
TO OVERSELL TRIPE
RESPELL RIOT VOTE
RESPELL VETO RIOT
RESOLVE TO TRIPLE
OR VIOLET RESPELT
OR VIOLET RESLEPT

LOVE TRIO RESPELT
OR VIOLET PETRELS
SILVER PETREL TOO
VILE PETREL ROOST
OR PI LOVE LETTERS
LIVE POOR LETTERS
TO POLITER REVELS
OVER LETTER SPOIL
SETTLE RIVER LOOP
SETTLE PRIOR LOVE
TILT LOVER REPOSE
LO SILVER TREETOP
ROLL OVER IT STEEP
POOR LITTLE VERSE
LOOT TRIPLE VERSE
TIPTOE VERSE ROLL
TO OVERSPILL TREE
TELL TREE PROVISO
EVER SPOTLIT ROLE
TO RIVER EELS PLOT
SILVER PETREL TOO
PROVE LETTER SOIL
PROVE TITLE ROLES

Opposite
List of anagrams for Liverpool
Street, a selection of which are
used in *Eastbound*.

Right
Cover of Ludwig Wittgenstein's
book *Remarks on Colour*.

Below
Found old postcard of White
City, the site of the *Franco-British
Exhibition* in 1908. All of the
buildings were clad in white marble
hence the name "White City".

Overleaf
Design of a page from Ludwig
Wittgenstein's book *Remarks
on Colour*.

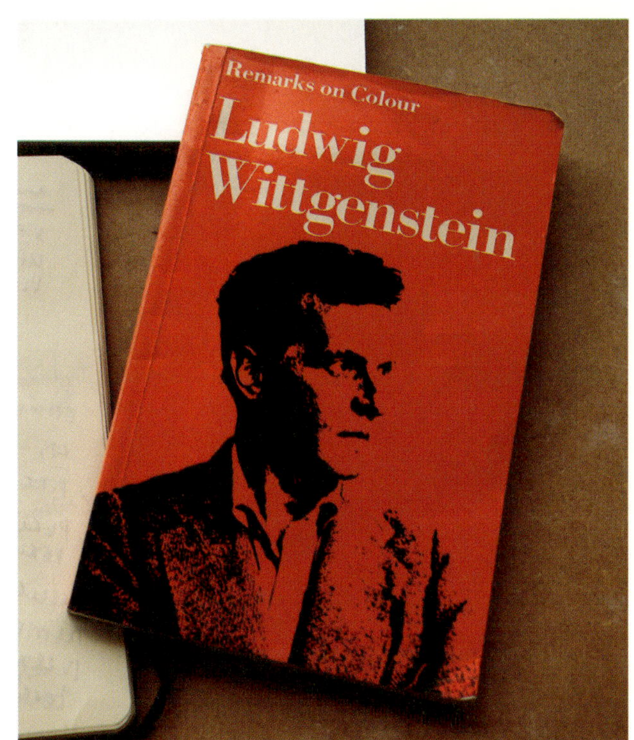

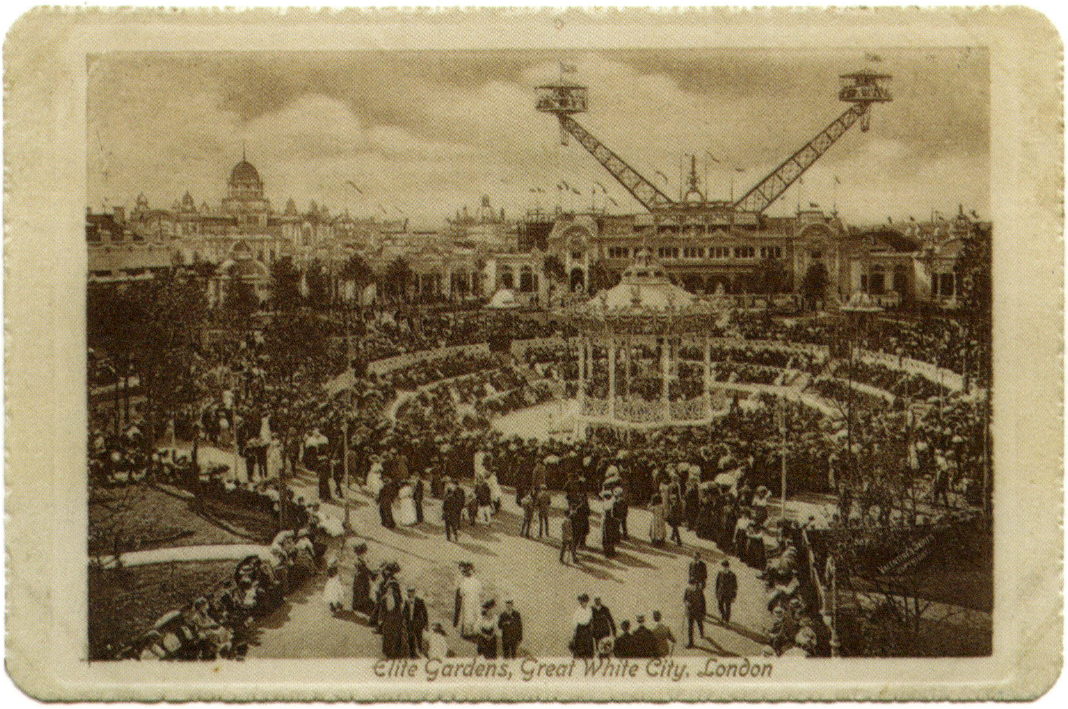

1. Ein Sprachspiel: Darüber berichten, ob ein bestimmter Körper heller oder dunkler als ein andrer sei. — Aber nun gibt es ein verwandtes: Über das Verhältnis der Helligkeiten bestimmter Farbtöne aussagen. (Damit ist zu vergleichen: Das Verhältnis der Längen zweier Stäbe bestimmen — und das Verhältnis zweier Zahlen bestimmen.) — Die Form der Sätze in beiden Sprachspielen ist die gleiche "X ist heller als Y". Aber im ersten ist es eine externe Relation und der Satz zeitlich, im zweiten ist es eine interne Relation und der Satz zeitlos.

2. In einem Bild, in welchem ein Stück weißes Papier seine Helligkeit vom blauen Himmel kriegt, ist dieser heller als das weiße Papier. Und doch ist in einem andern Sinne Blau die dunklere, Weiß die hellere Farbe. (Goethe). Auf der Palette ist das Weiß die hellste Farbe.

3. Lichtenberg sagt, nur wenige Menschen hätten je reines Weiß gesehen. So verwenden also die Meisten das Wort falsch? Und wie hat *er* den richtigen Gebrauch gelernt? — Er hat nach dem gewöhnlichen Gebrauch einen idealen konstruiert. Und das heißt nicht, einen bessern, sondern einen in gewisser Richtung verfeinerten, worin etwas auf die Spitze getrieben wird.

4. Und freilich kann ein so konstruierter uns wieder über den tatsächlichen Gebrauch belehren.

5. Wenn ich von einem Papier sage, es sei rein weiß, und es würde Schnee neben das Papier gehalten und dieses sähe nun grau aus, so würde ich es in seiner normalen Umgebung doch mit Recht weiß, nicht hellgrau, nennen. Es könnte sein, daß ich, im Laboratorium etwa, einen verfeinerten Begriff von Weiß verwendete (wie z.B. auch einen verfeinerten Begriff der genauen Zeitbestimmung).

6. Was läßt sich dafür sagen, daß Grün eine primäre Farbe ist, keine Mischfarbe von Blau und Gelb? Wäre es richtig zu sagen: "Man kann das nur unmittelbar erkennen, indem man die Farben betrachtet?" Aber wie weiß ich, daß ich dasselbe mit den Worten

I

A language-game: Report whether a certain body is lighter or
darker than another. — But now there's a related one: State the relationship between the lightness of certain shades of colour. (Compare
with this: Determining the relationship between the lengths of two
sticks — and the relationship between two numbers.) — The form of the
propositions in both language-games is the same: "X is lighter than
Y". But in the first it is an external relation and the proposition is
temporal, in the second it is an internal relation and the proposition
is timeless.

In a picture in which a piece of white paper gets its lightness
from the blue sky, the sky is lighter than the white paper. And yet in
another sense blue is the darker and white the lighter colour.
(Goethe). On the palette white is the lightest colour.

Lichtenberg says that very few people have ever seen pure white.
So do most people use the word wrong, then? And how did *he*
learn the correct use? — He constructed an ideal use from the ordinary
one. And that is not to say a better one, but one that has been refined
along certain lines and in the process something has been carried to
extremes.

And of course such a construct may in turn teach us something
about the way we in fact use the word.

If I say a piece of paper is pure white, and if snow were placed
next to it and it then appeared grey, in its normal surroundings I
would still be right in calling it white and not light grey. It could be
that I use a more refined concept of white in, say, a laboratory
(where, for example, I also use a more refined concept of precise
determination of time).

What is there in favor of saying that green is a primary colour,
not a blend of blue and yellow? Would it be right to say: "You can
only know it directly by looking at the colours"? But how do I know
that I mean the same by the words "primary colours" as some other

Alice Channer

Hard Metal Body, 2012
Notting Hill Gate Underground station

Describing her works as "figurative sculptures without a body", Alice
Channer often conceives her sculptures, exhibitions and works on
paper around the idea of a virtual body—whether the body of the
room or that of the viewer—in an attempt to inhabit or dress the
spaces in which her works are shown.

    Hard Metal Body was made in direct response to the cold and
detached metal surfaces of the tunnel where the work was installed,
in relation to the soft human bodies of the commuters who use the
station. Observing them going up and down the escalators that take
them through the tunnel, Channer was attracted to their arms, the
most animated parts of their bodies in that context. The resulting
work tried both to confuse and define the edges between human and
non-human entities. A succession of rough ellipses on a pastel blue
background, varying in size, were installed on each stretch of wall on
either side of the escalators. These rings were the detailed imprints,
reproduced on vinyl, of elastic waistbands from clothing. Through
this use of the stretchy clothing that we usually wear close to our
skin, Channer made indirect reference to the human body.

    Hard Metal Body was produced by cutting out the waistbands,
manually rolling ink over them and then pressing them against paper.
The results of this primitive printing method were digitally scanned and
manipulated, and then reproduced on vinyl that was installed on the
wall. At the end of the process, the details of the imprint were so clear
that the flattened-down waistbands still evoked the original 3-D objects.

    For Channer, volume in objects is paradoxically evoked through
flat surfaces, and *vice versa*. This often results in artworks that
can disorient the viewer's sense of shape and flatness. In the work
Breathing, 2011, for example, she made solid aluminium casts of
similar stretch waistbands and hung them from the wall on wooden
dowels. These objects are so elongated and flattened that they are
almost two-dimensional. In the work titled *Eyes and Lungs*, 2011,
she made ink prints from her arm. The arm prints were scanned,
stretched and reprinted onto Spandex fabric, which was then wrapped
around aluminium frames attached perpendicular to two 20-metre
long walls. In this way, the artist in a sense stretched her arm to the
length of the room.

    A text excerpt included at the end of this section offers an insight
into her recent fascination with the fantasy, currently voiced by some
scientists, that the body could become pure virtual information in
the very near future. *Hard Metal Body* is a playful continuation of

Opposite and Overleaf
Alice Channer, *Hard Metal Body*,
2012. Notting Hill Gate
Underground station.

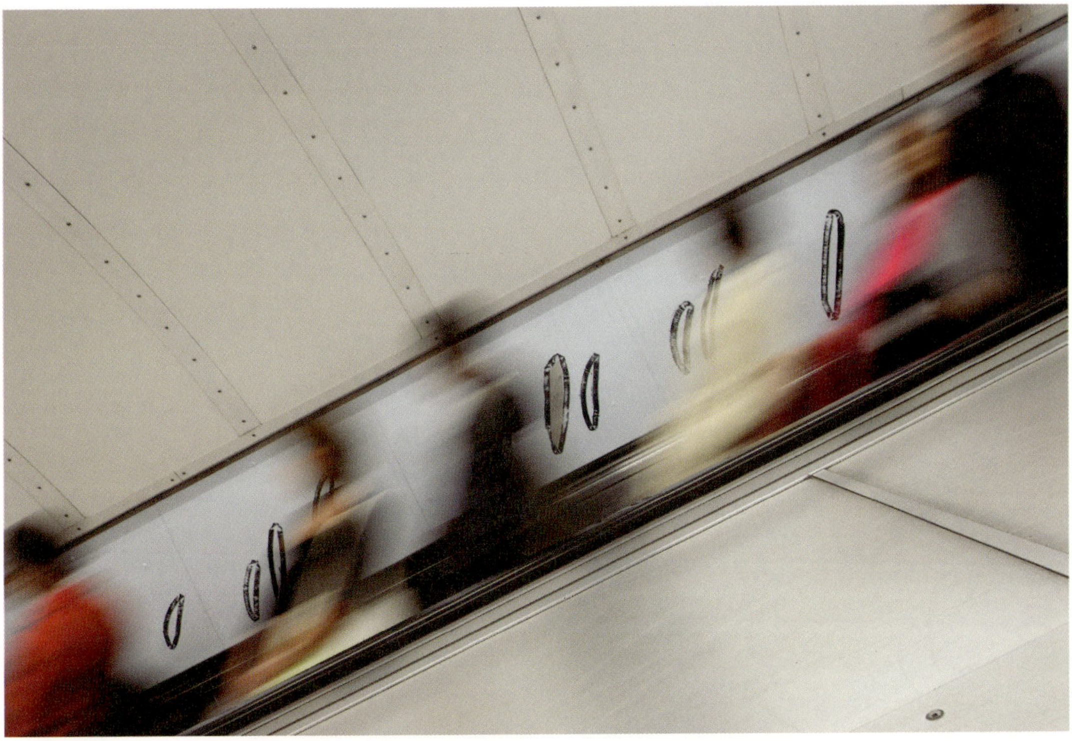

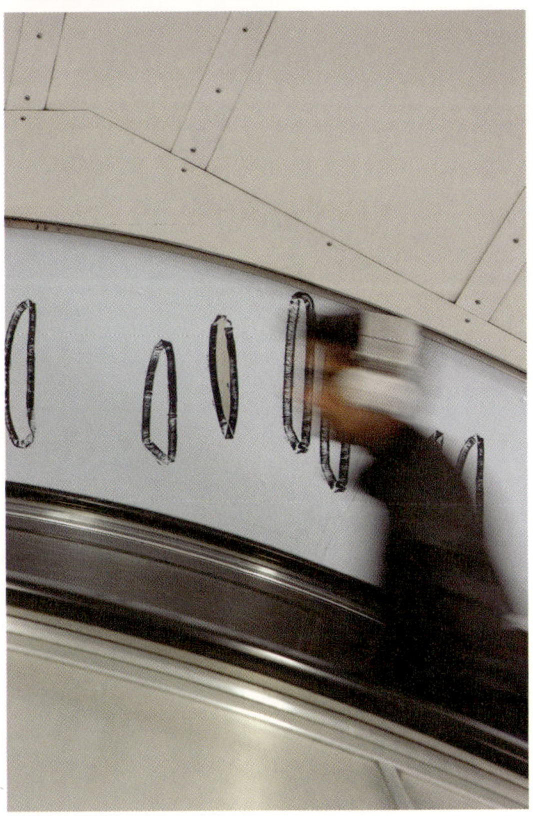
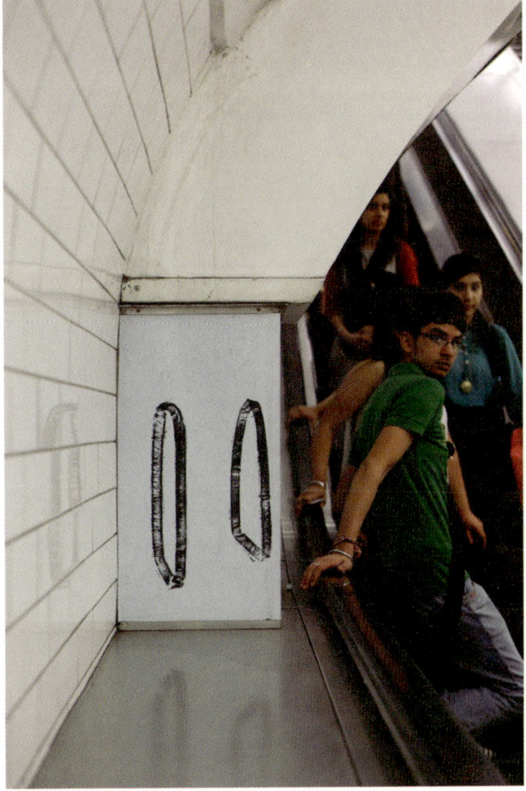

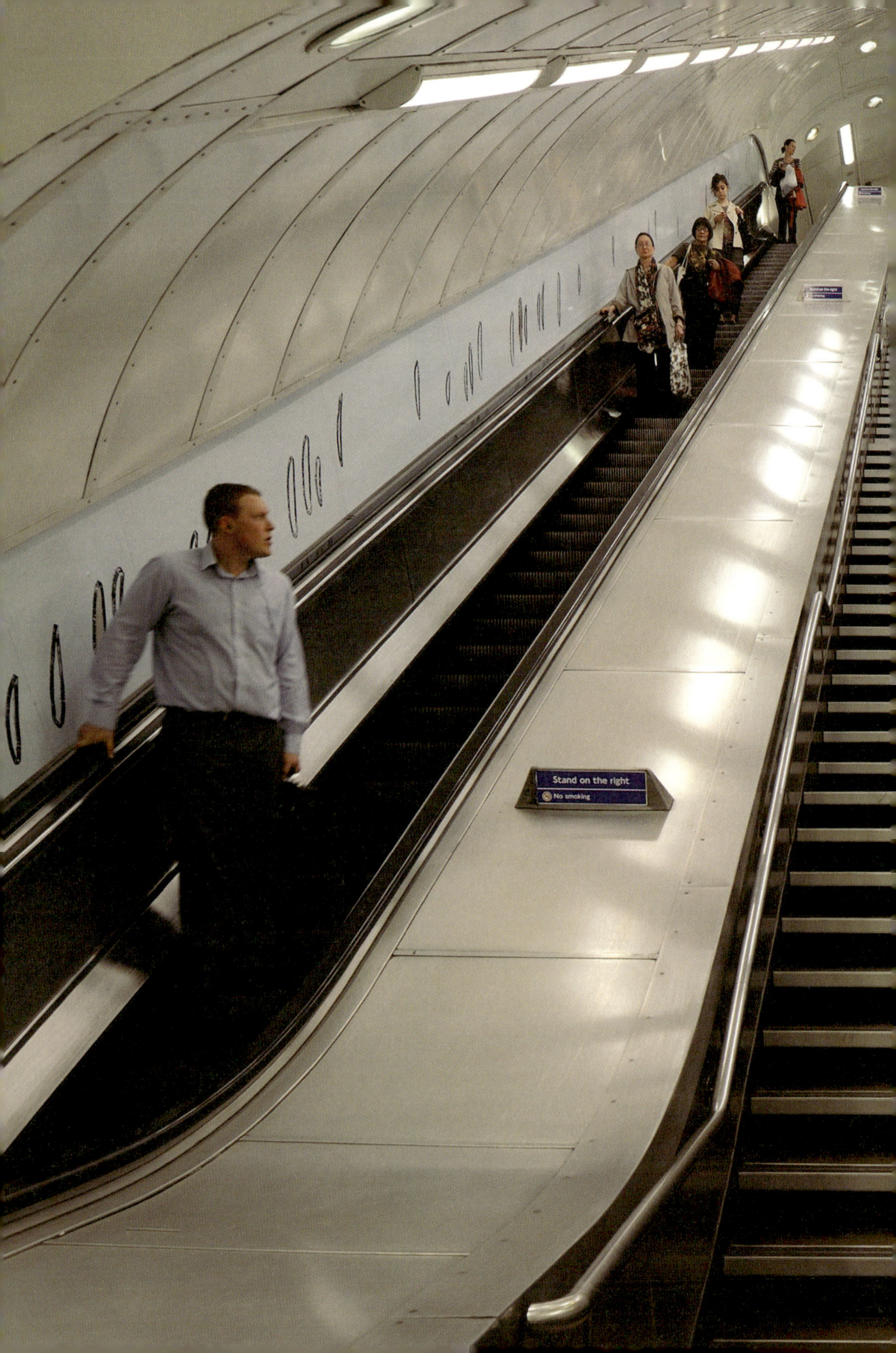

Stand on the right
No smoking

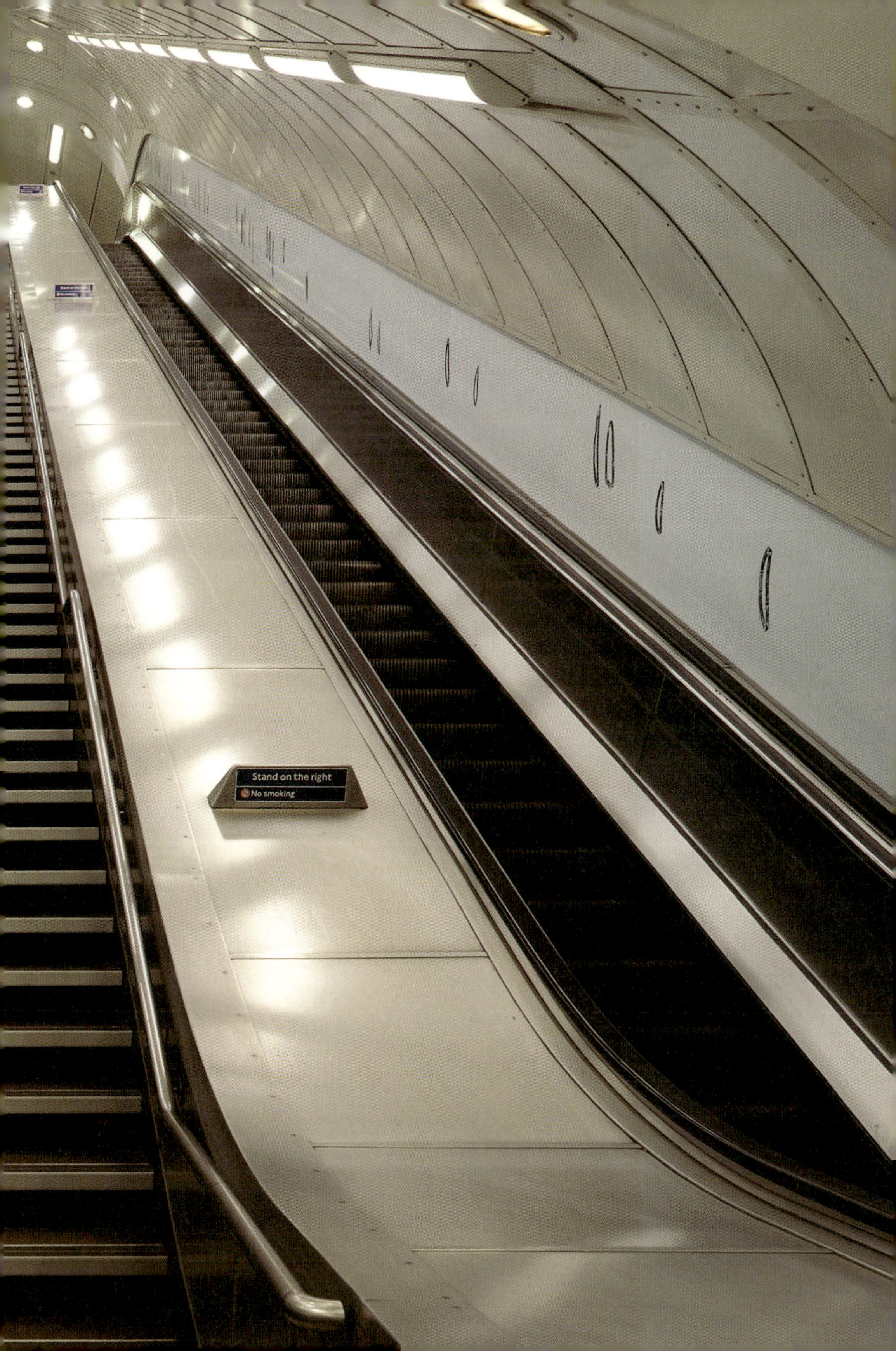

Stand on the right
No smoking

her interest in pinpointing a new human subjectivity defined by the industrial and post-industrial materials and techniques that constitute our late-capitalist era. As Channer says, it is almost as if the plastic processes that shape and form her works "are authored by many different beings, and only one of these is me".

Alice Channer (born in UK, 1977) lives and works in London. She graduated in 2008 with an MA in Sculpture from the Royal College of Art, London, following a BA in Fine Art from Goldsmiths College, London, in 2006. Recent solo exhibitions include *Out Of Body*, South London Gallery, UK, 2012; *Body-Conscious*, The Approach, London, UK, 2011 and *Other-Directed*, BolteLang, Zurich, Switzerland, 2011. Her works have been part of many group exhibitions, including: *The London Open*, Whitechapel Gallery, London, UK, 2012; *Caroline Achaintre, Sara Barker, Alice Channer*, Eastside Projects, Birmingham, UK, 2012; *Young London*, V22 Workspace, London, UK, 2011 and *Unto This Last*, Raven Row, London, UK, 2010.

Alice Channer, *Breathing*, 2012.

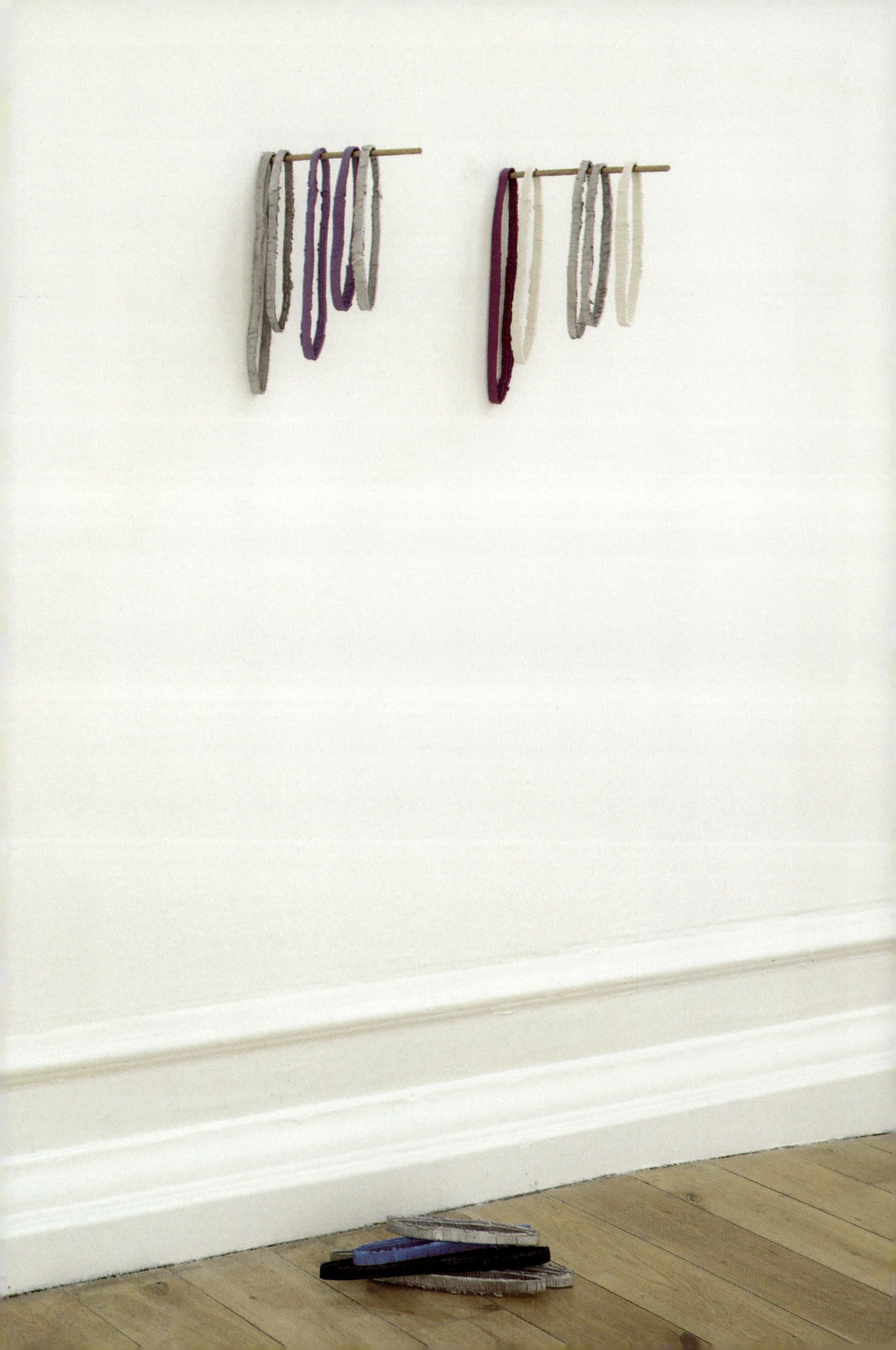

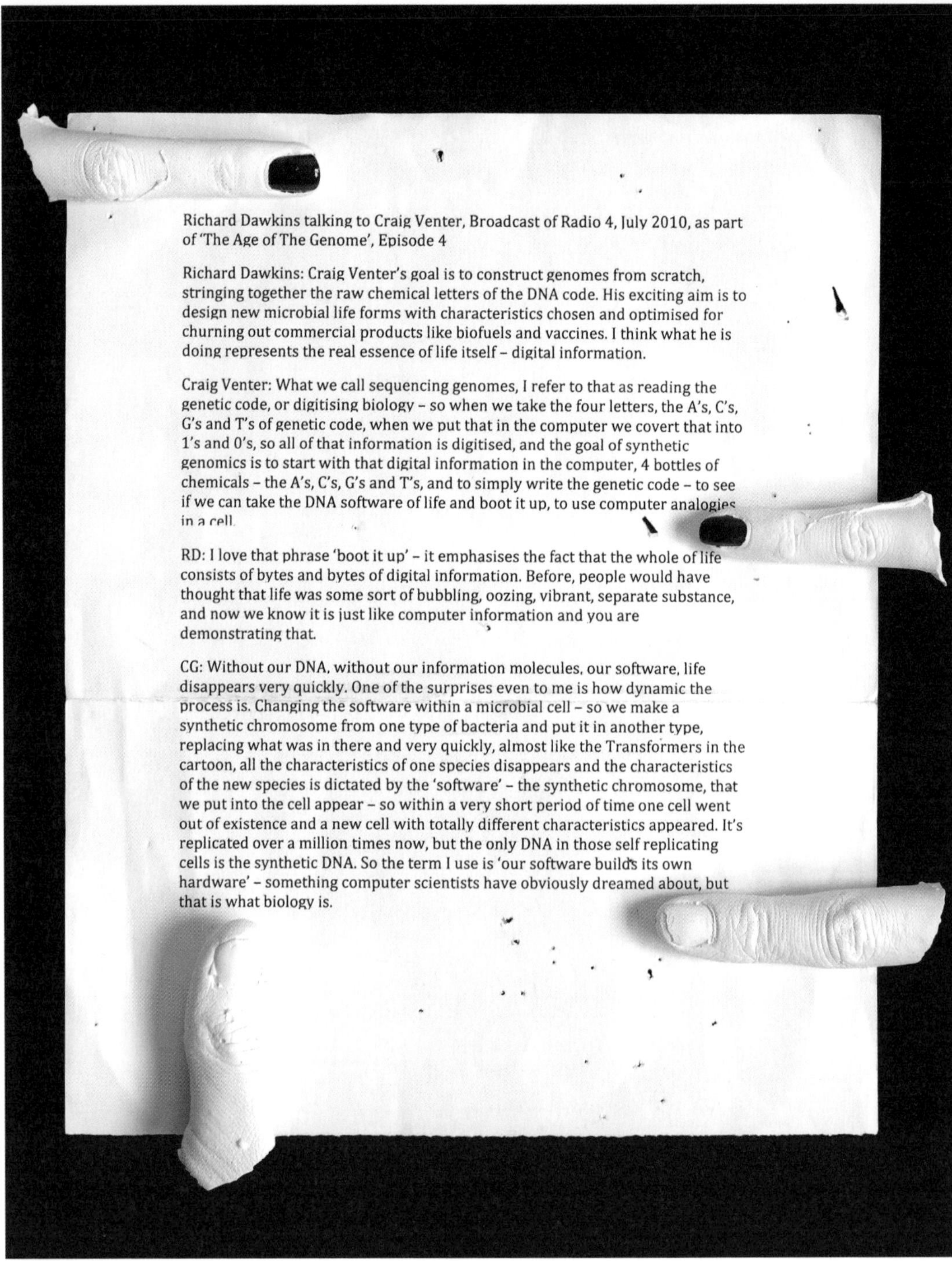

Richard Dawkins talking to Craig Venter, Broadcast of Radio 4, July 2010, as part of 'The Age of The Genome', Episode 4

Richard Dawkins: Craig Venter's goal is to construct genomes from scratch, stringing together the raw chemical letters of the DNA code. His exciting aim is to design new microbial life forms with characteristics chosen and optimised for churning out commercial products like biofuels and vaccines. I think what he is doing represents the real essence of life itself – digital information.

Craig Venter: What we call sequencing genomes, I refer to that as reading the genetic code, or digitising biology – so when we take the four letters, the A's, C's, G's and T's of genetic code, when we put that in the computer we covert that into 1's and 0's, so all of that information is digitised, and the goal of synthetic genomics is to start with that digital information in the computer, 4 bottles of chemicals – the A's, C's, G's and T's, and to simply write the genetic code – to see if we can take the DNA software of life and boot it up, to use computer analogies in a cell.

RD: I love that phrase 'boot it up' – it emphasises the fact that the whole of life consists of bytes and bytes of digital information. Before, people would have thought that life was some sort of bubbling, oozing, vibrant, separate substance, and now we know it is just like computer information and you are demonstrating that.

CG: Without our DNA, without our information molecules, our software, life disappears very quickly. One of the surprises even to me is how dynamic the process is. Changing the software within a microbial cell – so we make a synthetic chromosome from one type of bacteria and put it in another type, replacing what was in there and very quickly, almost like the Transformers in the cartoon, all the characteristics of one species disappears and the characteristics of the new species is dictated by the 'software' – the synthetic chromosome, that we put into the cell appear – so within a very short period of time one cell went out of existence and a new cell with totally different characteristics appeared. It's replicated over a million times now, but the only DNA in those self replicating cells is the synthetic DNA. So the term I use is 'our software builds its own hardware' – something computer scientists have obviously dreamed about, but that is what biology is.

Extract from a talk between Richard Dawkins and Craig Venter on Radio 4 as part of "The Age of The Genome", Episode 4, July 2010.

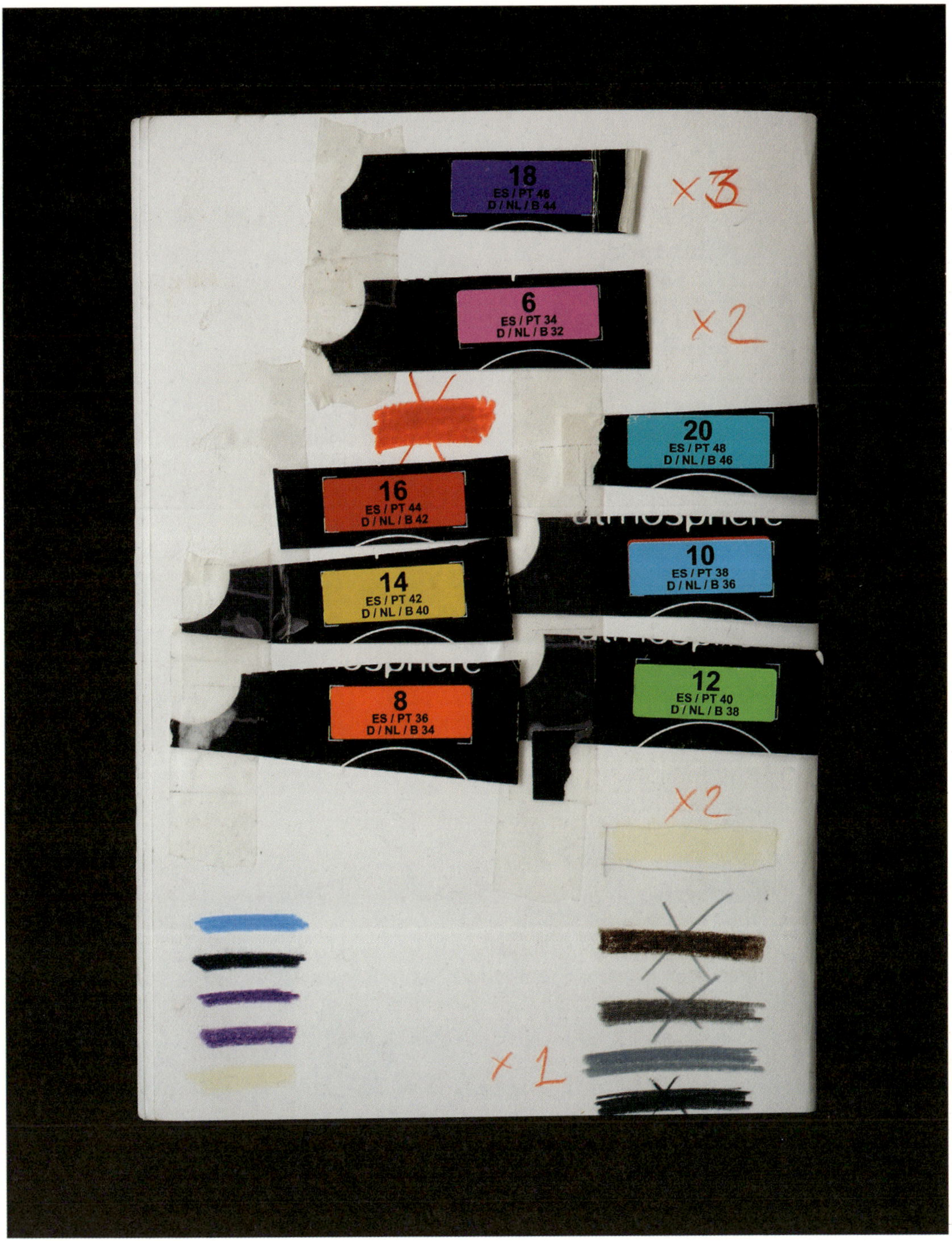

A page from Alice Channer's
sketchbook in preparation for
Breathing, 2012.

Bob and Roberta Smith
and Tim Newton

Who is Community?, 2012
Stratford Underground station

Who is Community? was a collaboration between Bob and Roberta Smith and Tim Newton. Smith has worked in a variety of media including painting, performance, sculpture, film and installation. He is known for employing DIY methods—including painting on pieces of scrap wood—drawing on a number of influences from punk to folk in order to personalise political sloganeering. Newton is a film director whose short film *Trimming Pablo*, 2011, which featured a cameo from Smith, is a fictionalised account of Pablo Picasso's visit to the 1950 Sheffield Peace Congress.

Who is Community? involved the production of a film that tells the story of a fictional romance between Pierre de Coubertin, father of the modern Olympics, and the German theorist Hannah Arendt. The project also included a number of large artworks on display in Stratford Underground station. Originally painted by Smith, they featured characters and ideas from the film. Cut-out figures of Arendt and de Coubertin also appeared at cultural venues around Stratford.

The film was set in modern-day Stratford, the main site of the 2012 London Olympic and Paralympics Games. Although Coubertin, a French aristocrat born in 1863, never met Arendt, in imagining an encounter between the two, the artists invite the idea that there may have been a synergy between their beliefs.
Born into a family of secular German Jews in 1906, Arendt is known for her ideas on freedom as something that is constructed in the community, while Coubertin was interested in the potential of sport to create "moral and social strength". In founding an international sports festival at a moment when the world was coming out of a series of global conflicts, he established a legacy that remains today: the maintenance of peace through athletic competition.

The film draws upon the cinematic style of silent comedies and makes particular reference to the early 1900s, featuring the Art Deco architecture of Loughton Underground station, and clothing the Olympic athletes (who live in Coubertin's moustache!) in turn-of-the-century costume. It was also shown on a specially designed structure in Stratford station, which was modelled after an original ticket kiosk installed at Hainault station in 1948. Known as passimeters, the kiosks were introduced in the early 1920s.

Bob and Roberta Smith and Tim Newton, *Who is Community?*, 2012. Artwork at Stratford East Picture House.

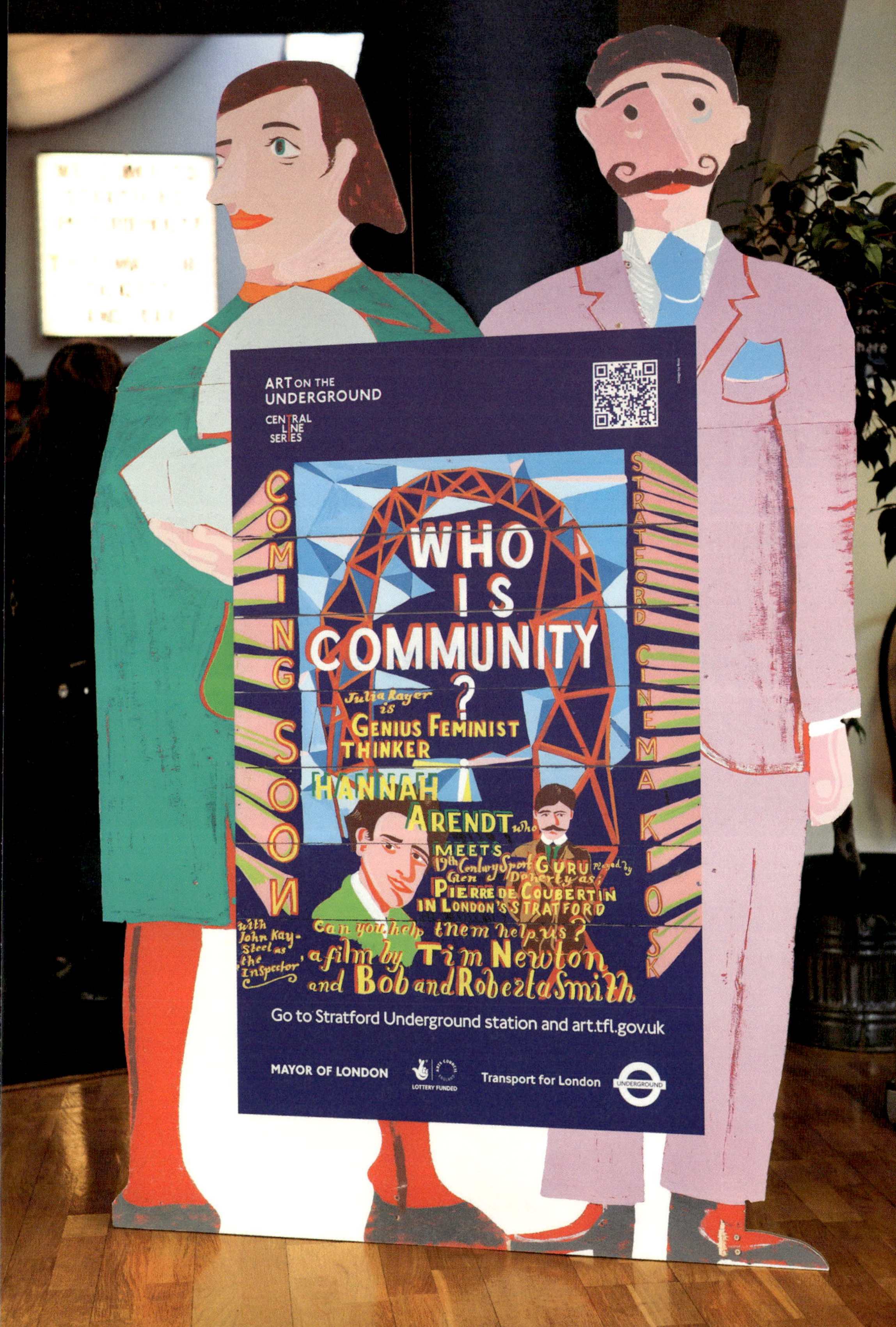

ART ON THE UNDERGROUND
CENTRAL LINE SERIES
COMING SOON
STRATFORD CINEMA KIOSK
WHO IS COMMUNITY ?
Julia Rayer is GENIUS FEMINIST THINKER
HANNAH ARENDT who
MEETS 19th Century Sport GURU played by
Glen Doherty as
PIERRE DE COUBERTIN
IN LONDON'S STRATFORD
with John Kay-Steel as the "Inspector"
can you help them help us ?
a film by TIM NEWTON
and Bob and Roberta Smith
Go to Stratford Underground station and art.tfl.gov.uk
MAYOR OF LONDON
LOTTERY FUNDED
Transport for London
UNDERGROUND

Bob and Roberta Smith (born in UK, 1963) studied art at the University of Reading, and was awarded a scholarship to The British School in Rome, which he followed with an MA at Goldsmith's College, London. He has had more than 15 solo shows to date. In 2007, his sculpture proposal was shortlisted for the fourth plinth in Trafalgar Square. In 2008, he collaborated with Electric Pedals to create an interactive Christmas tree for Tate Britain and in 2009 he contributed to the Tate Triennial exhibition *Altermodern*.

Before moving into film production, Tim Newton (born in UK, 1962) worked extensively as an actor, playwright and street performer, specialising in physical theatre. His solo show *The Ballad of the Limehouse Rat* won four London Theatre awards. He also regularly performed in plays by Ken Campbell, including *The Warp* and *Makbed*. He has produced and directed TV commercials, viral videos and several factual entertainment series for BBC and ITV, including *Beat the Burglar* and *Cash in the Attic*. He continues to make his own independent films.

Bob and Roberta Smith and Tim Newton, *Who is Community?*, 2012. Stratford Underground station.

Overleaf
Bob and Roberta Smith and Tim Newton, *Who is Community?*, 2012. Production stills.

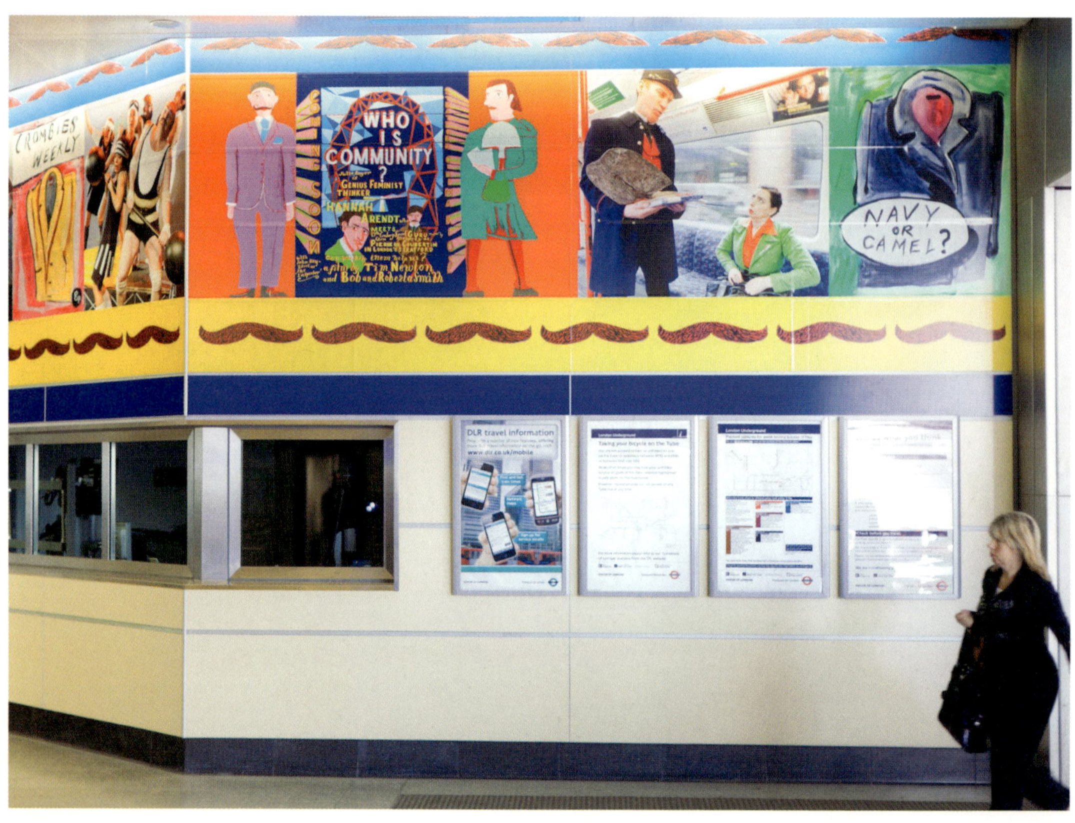

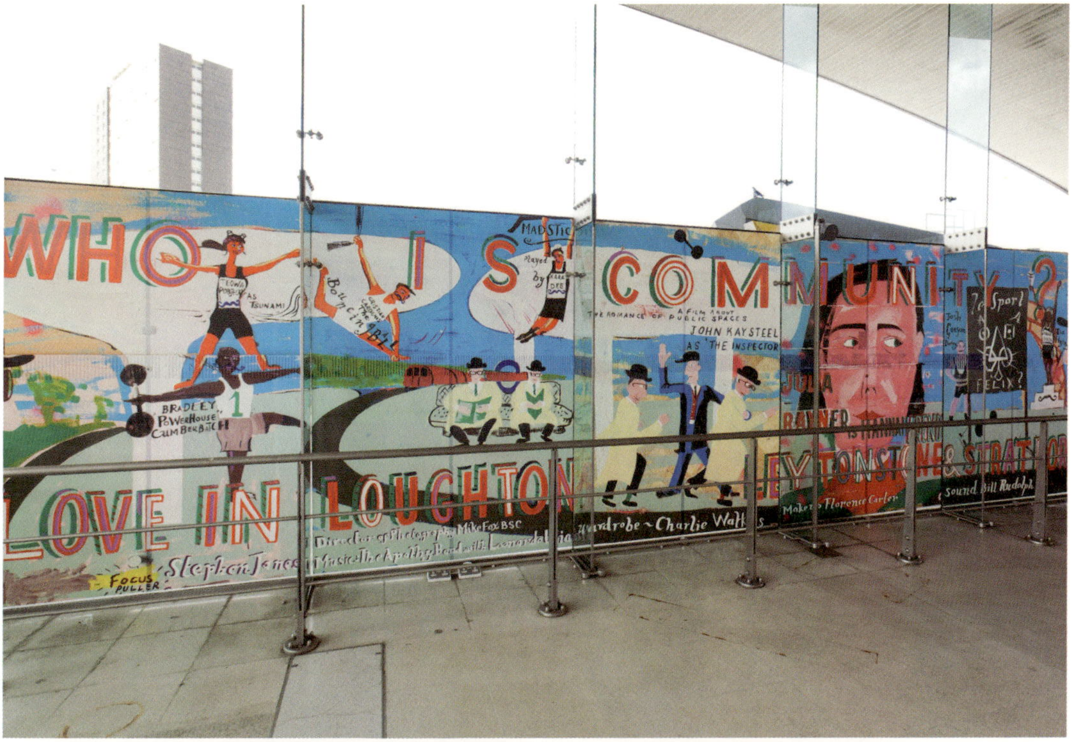

WHO IS COMMUNITY?
MAD STIC
A FILM ABOUT
THE ROMANCE OF PUBLIC SPACES
JOHN KAY STEEL
AS 'THE INSPECTOR'
BRADLEY
POWERHOUSE
CUMBERBATCH
LOVE IN LOUGHTON
LEYTONSTONE & STRATFORD
Directors of Photography Mike Fox BSC
Wardrobe ~ Charlie Watts
Maker Florence Carter
Sound Bill Rudolph
Focus Puller
Stephen Jones
Sport A FELIX?
JULIA RAYNER

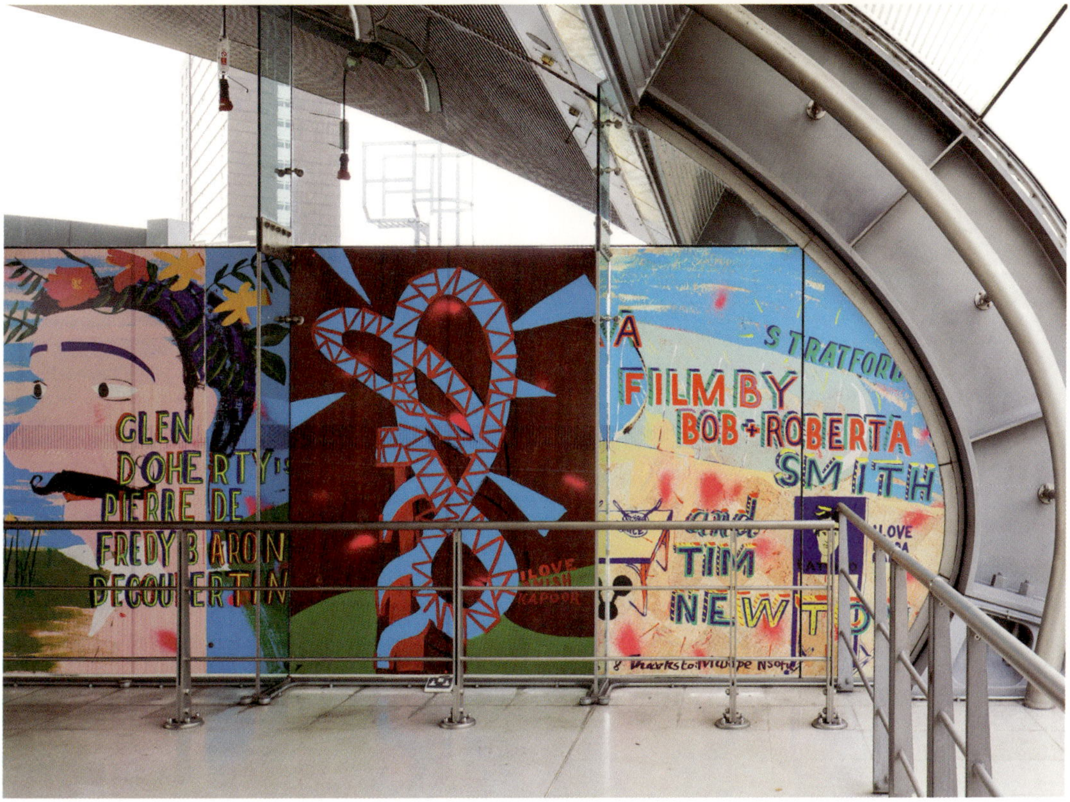

GLEN
D'OHERTY
PIERRE DE
FREDY BARON
DECOUBERTIN
A FILM BY
BOB + ROBERTA
SMITH
and
TIM NEWTON
STRATFORD
LOVE
KAPOOR

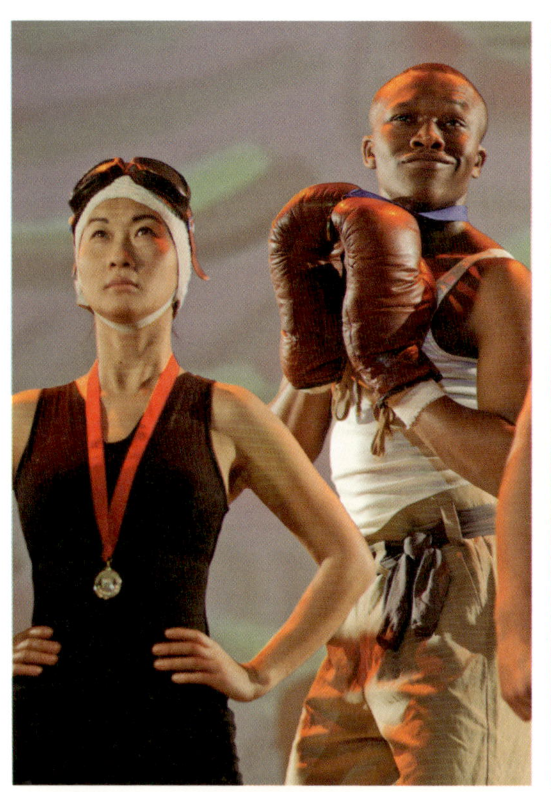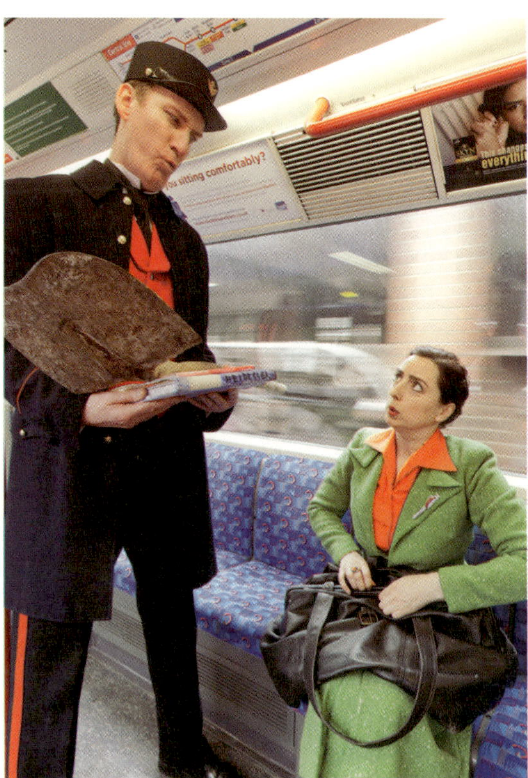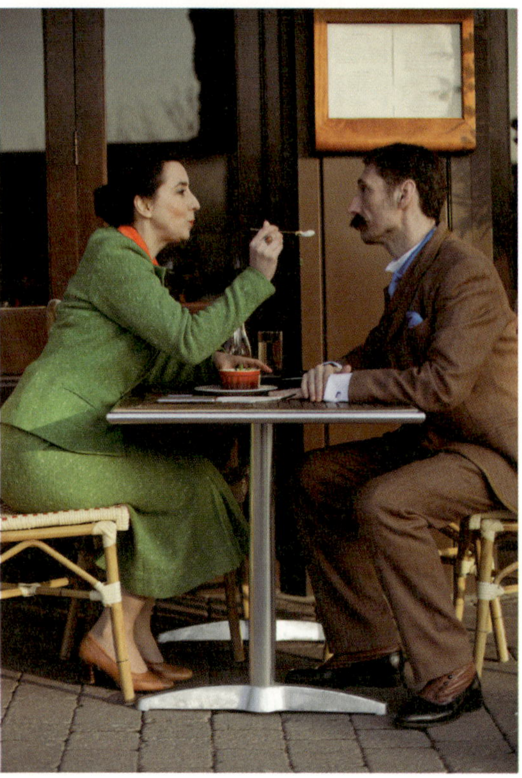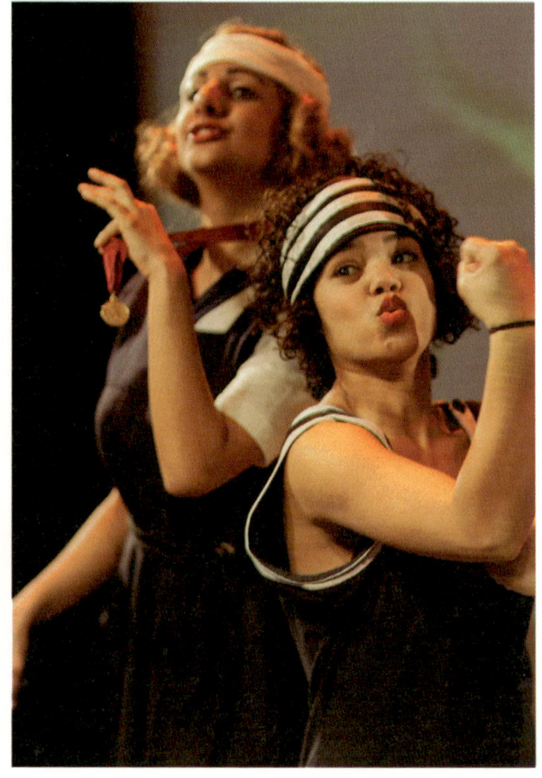

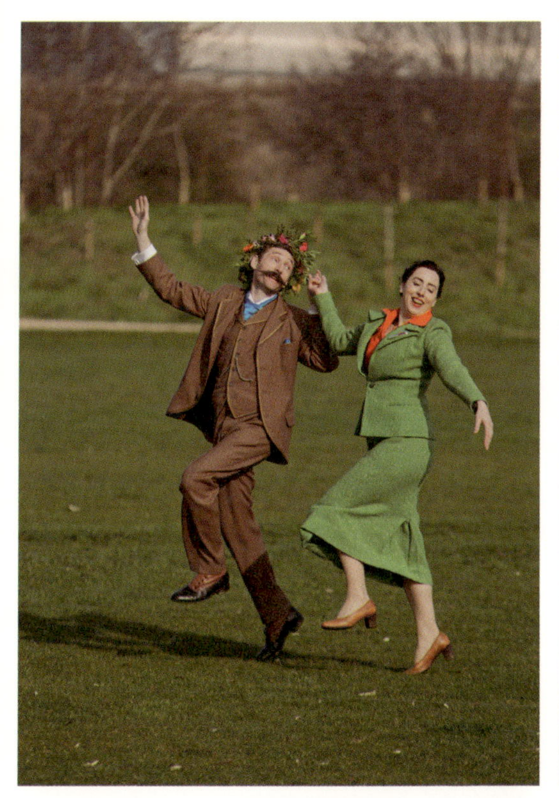

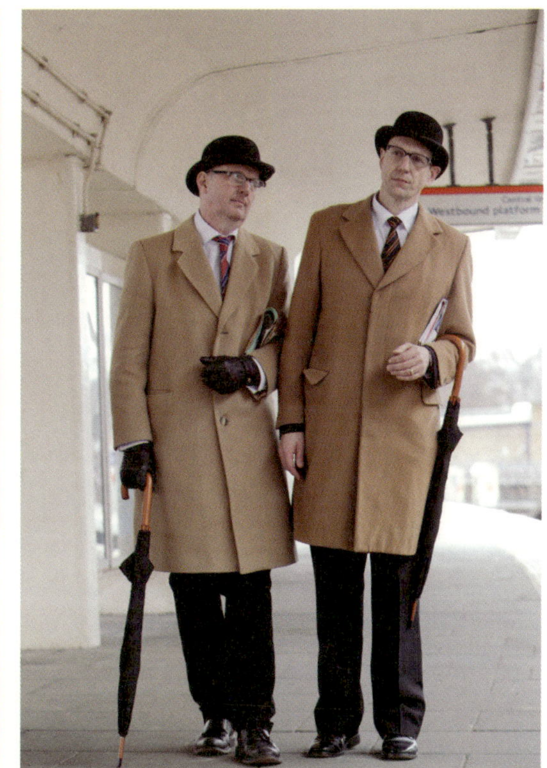

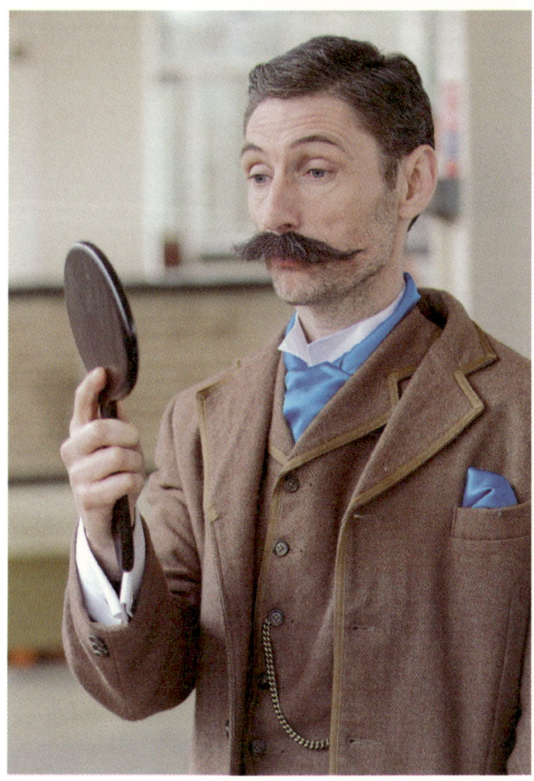

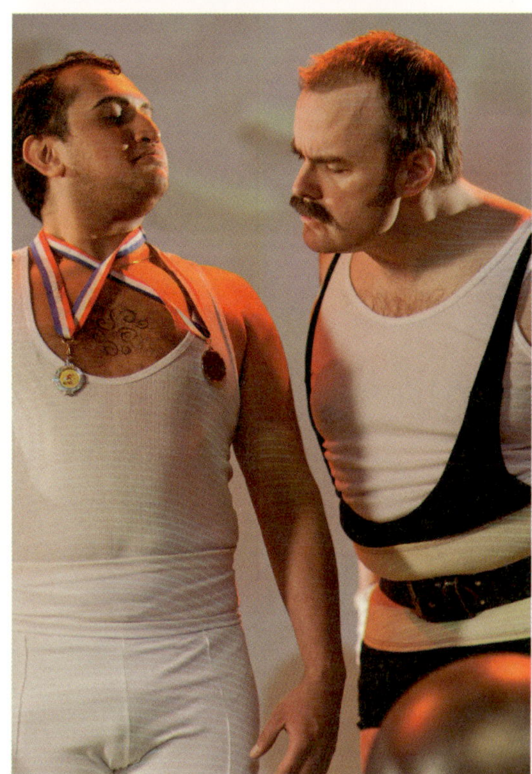

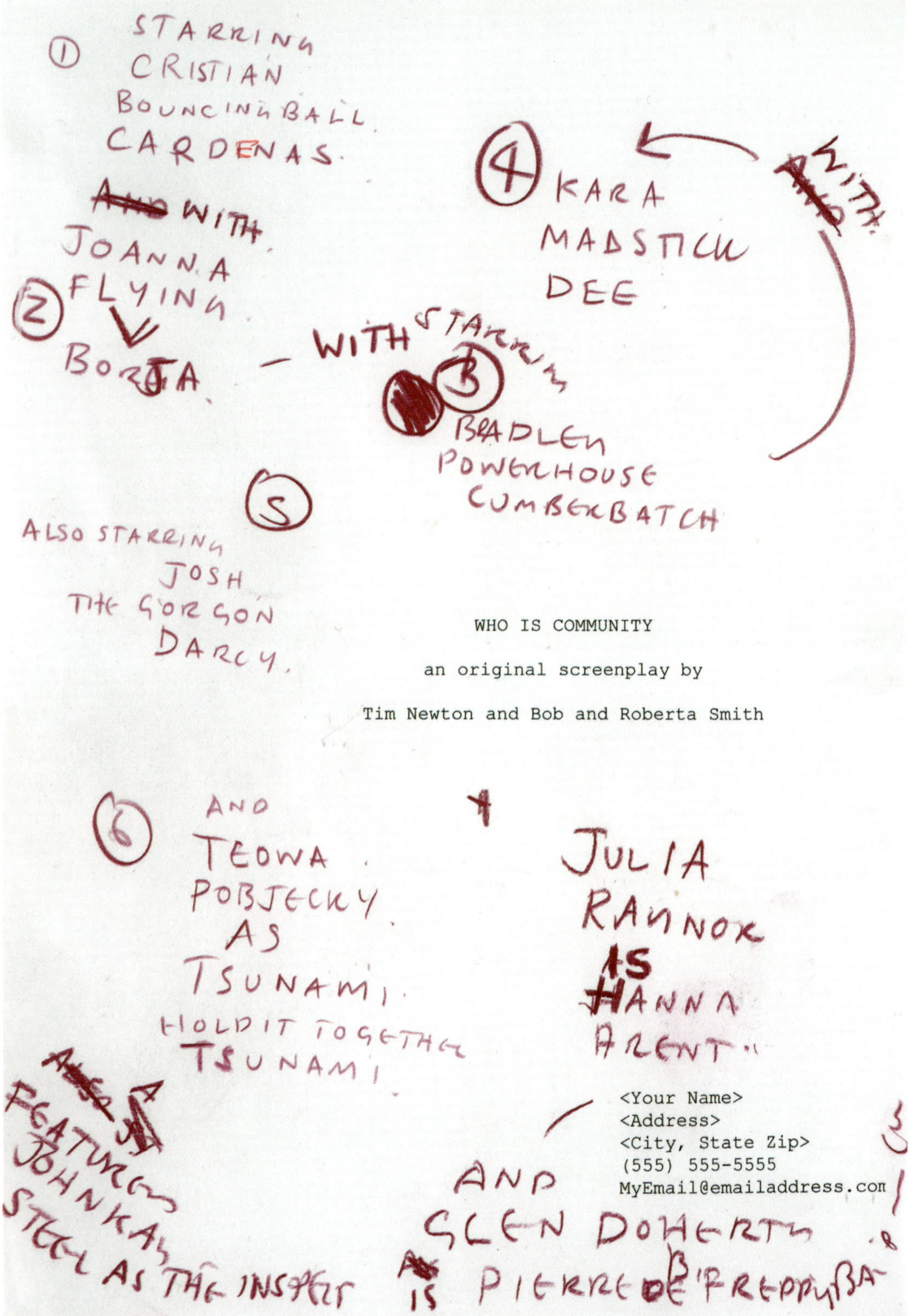

① STARRING
CRISTIAN
BOUNCING BALL
CARDENAS.

~~AND~~ WITH
JOANNA
② FLYING
BORTA.

— WITH STARRING

④ KARA
MADSTICK
DEE

~~WITH~~

③ BRADLEY
POWERHOUSE
CUMBERBATCH

⑤
ALSO STARRING
JOSH
THE GORGON
DARCY.

WHO IS COMMUNITY

an original screenplay by

Tim Newton and Bob and Roberta Smith

⑥ AND
TEOWA.
POBJECKY
AS
TSUNAMI.
HOLD IT TOGETHER
TSUNAMI.

JULIA
RANNOK
IS
~~HANNA~~
ARENT"

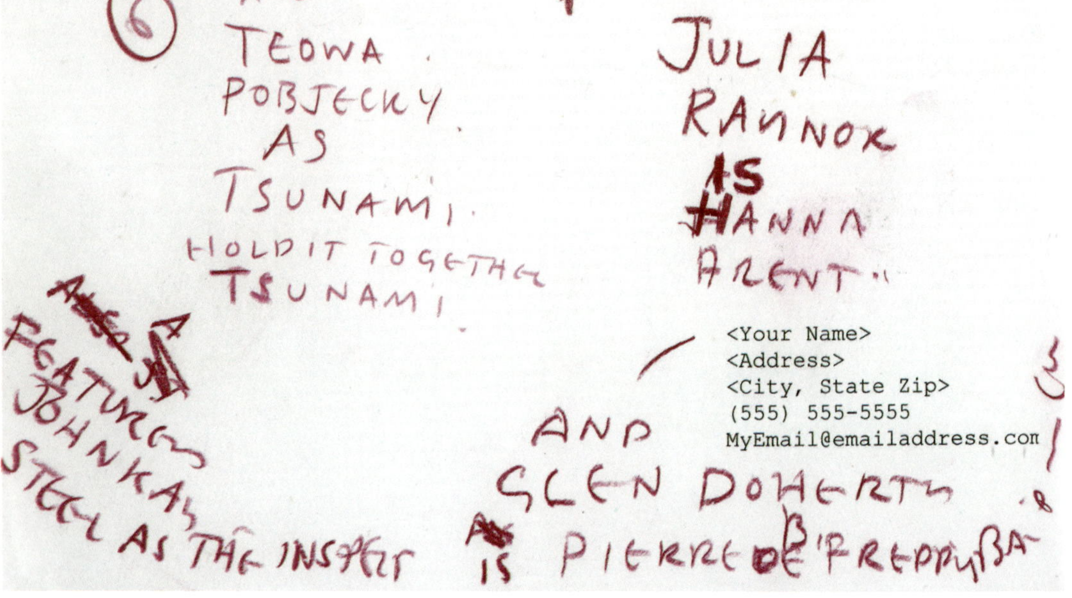

FEATURING
JOHNKA
STEEL AS THE INSPEC

AND
GLEN DOHERTY
AS PIERRE DE'FREDDYBAT
IS

80

The two mysterious men from Loughton Platform emerge on the brow of the hill - on the trail of Hannah. One of them suspiciously examines the flower he finds on the ground. The men sneer, disapproving.

                    BOB VO (CONT'D)
          Maybe deeper more positive feelings
          could be kindled. IS THIS A LOVE
          STORY?

Pierre and Hannah skip gaily along the Fatwalk, Coubertin wears a wreath of flowers on his head.

MEANWHILE...

The two mysterious men discover the olympic rings and cat-face that Pierre and Hannah drew earlier. One of them produces a small camera from his pocket and takes a photograph. The other spits into his pocket handkerchief and wipes the daubs away. Satisfied, the men move on.

                    BOB VO (CONT'D)
          Through our actions, our art and
          what we leave behind, human beings
          have the capacity to fall in love
          across many generations.

EXT. LEYTONSTONE STATION - DAY

                    BOB VO
          Personally, I love Frida Khalo.

PAINTING - FRIDA KAHLO - with her eponymous unibrow. It is mounted on a stand in the middle of the street.

Pierre and Hannah admire the painting. However, there's something different about Pierre at this moment - his moustache is gone. He suddenly realises - and removes Frida Kahlo's eyebrow from the painting.

He sticks the one large eyebrow under his nose and it transforms - via double exposure - to his familiar, handsome growth.

The couple smile and skip away.

EXT. PARISIENNE CAFE, LEYTONSTONE STATION - DAY

                                              FADE IN:

                    BOB VO
          Would Pierre de Frédy, Baron de
          Coubertin, have suggested a cup
          of coffee at the Parisienne cafe
          at Leytonstone station?

The couple sit sweetly at the table of the Parisienne cafe, making eyes.

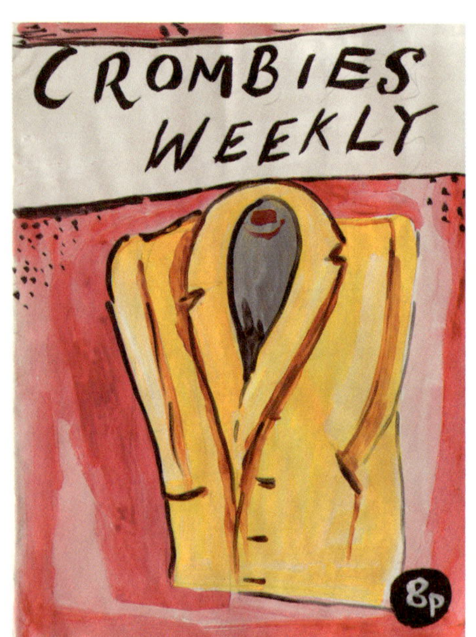
CROMBIES
WEEKLY
8p

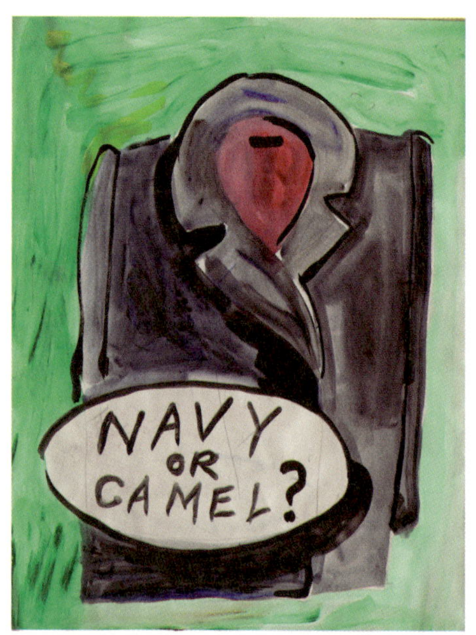
NAVY
OR
CAMEL?

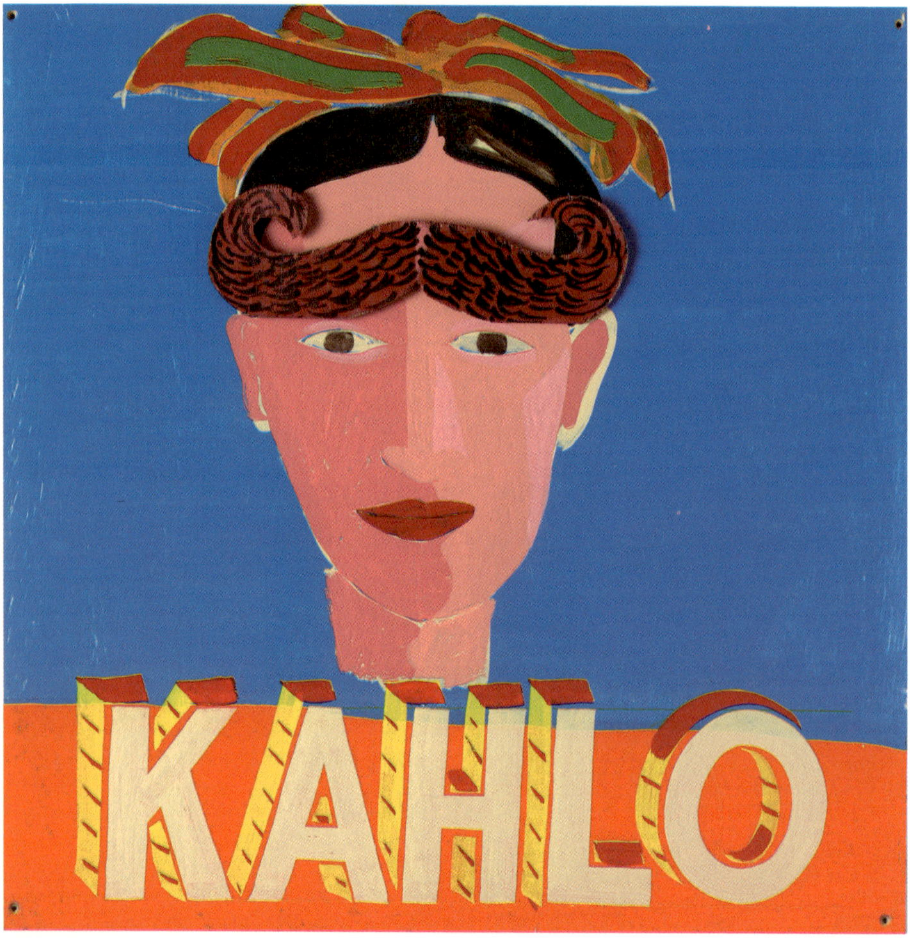

KAHLO

Previous pages
Bob and Roberta Smith and Tim Newton, *Who is Community?*, 2012. Pages from the original screenplay.

Opposite and Bottom
Bob and Roberta Smith and Tim Newton, *Who is Community?*, 2012. Props from the film.

Top
An original passimeter at Enfield West (now Oakwood) Underground station.

Middle
A sketch for the design of the *Stratford Cinema Kiosk* by Bob and Roberta Smith.

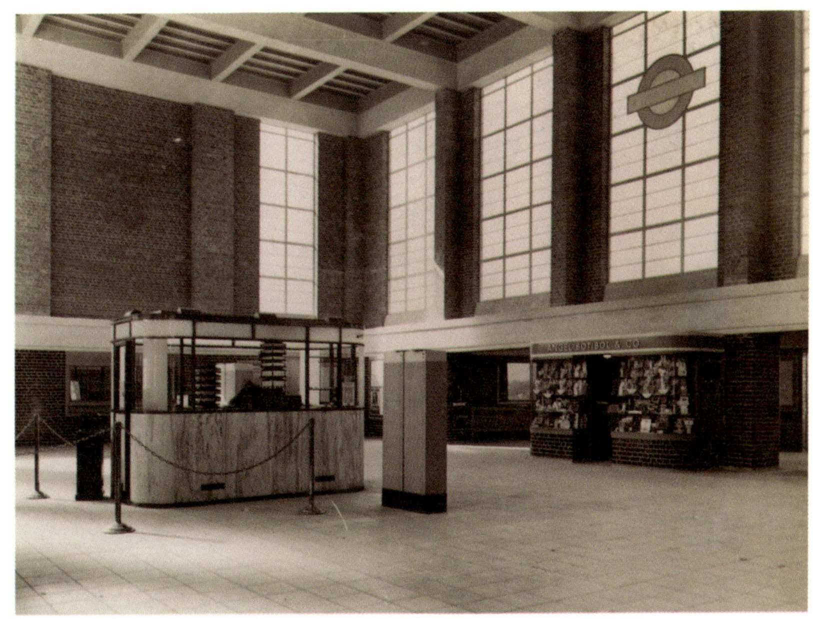

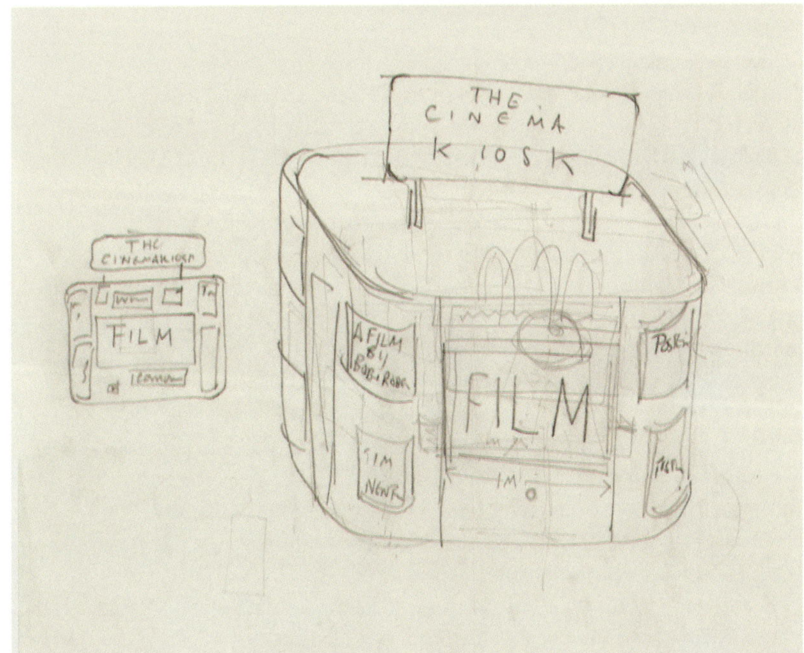

THE CINEMA KIOSK
THE CINEMAKIOSK
FILM
A FILM BY BOB+ROBR
FILM
TIM NEWR

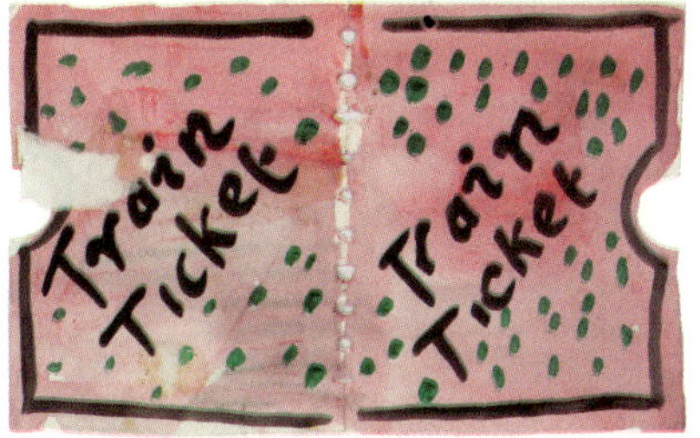

Train Ticket
Train Ticket

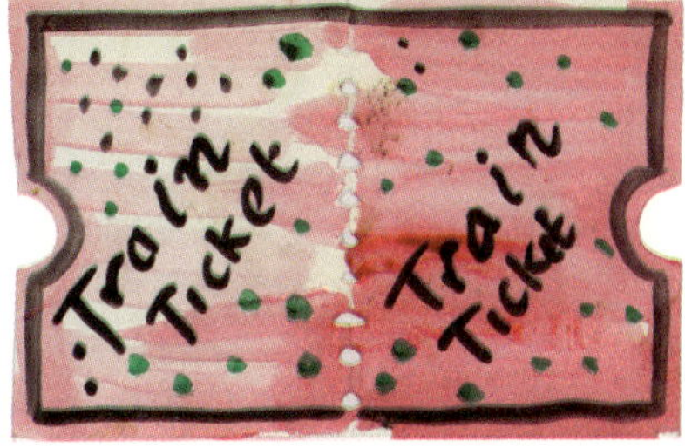

Train Ticket
Train Ticket

Public Programmes

Public discussions and events accompanied the launch of each project in the Central line series. Providing a platform to explore the ideas in the series, and each project, in greater detail, the events were also an opportunity to hear directly from the artists about their work.

In July 2011, Michael Landy participated in an in-conversation with Mark Vernon, a writer whose work primarily pursues the question: how to live? Vernon is the author of *The Meaning of Friendship* and *How to be an Agnostic*, and writes regularly for *The Guardian*, *TLS* and *The Evening Standard*, and broadcasts for the BBC. During the event, Landy and Vernon discussed the themes surrounding and influencing the *Acts of Kindness* project. The event was held in Toynbee Hall, in London's East End.

Later that summer, in late August, *A LOCK IS A GATE* launched at the V&A Museum of Childhood. The event was well-attended by over 30 young people aged nine –19 years from the Laburnum Boat Club youth project, on Regent's Canal in Hackney. As part of the launch, which included speeches by Ruth Ewan and Senior Youth Worker, Dominic Hinshelwood, an area was set up for guests to listen to the mini concept album.

At the end of March 2012, Anna Barham's *WHITE CITY* and Alice Channer's *Hard Metal Body* were jointly launched at the Gate Theatre, in Notting Hill. The two artists participated in a discussion about their work with art critic Rachel Withers. Drawing upon images of the work in-situ, the artists addressed what it was like making work in public space, similarities and differences between their work and their individual practices.

For the first time ever, an Art on the Underground commission, *Who is Community?*, was launched on the big screen, at Stratford East Picture House. Following screenings of previous works directed by Tim Newton, including *Trimming Pablo*, 2011 and *Leytonstone*, 2011, was the world premiere of *Who is Community?* After the screenings, the artists participated in a conversation about their work and took questions from the audience.

In addition, all of the artists in the Central line series were interviewed about their work and video podcasts about each project are available from the Art on the Underground website.

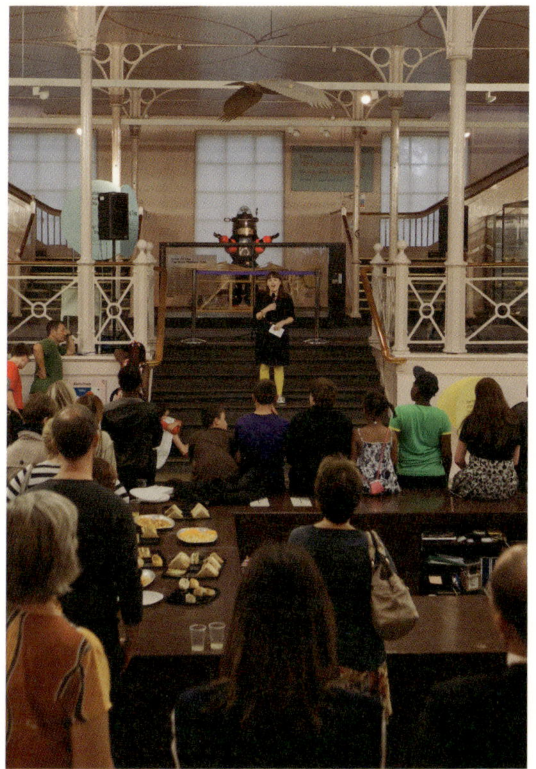

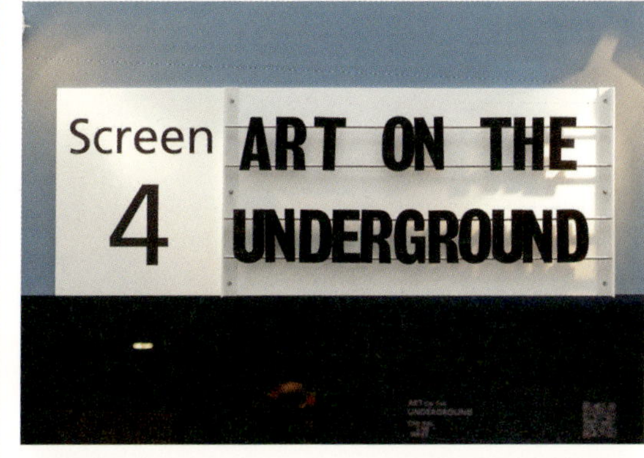

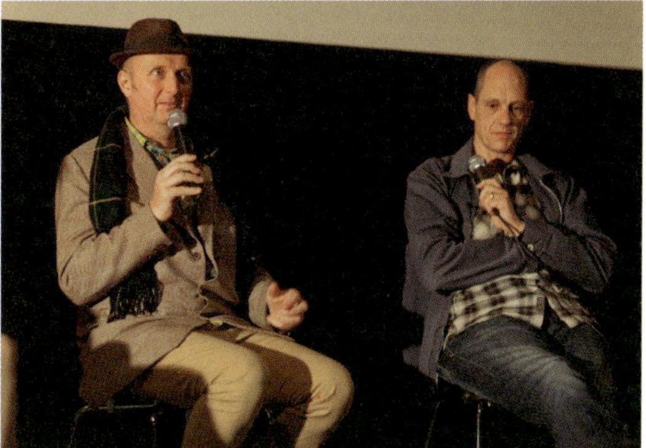

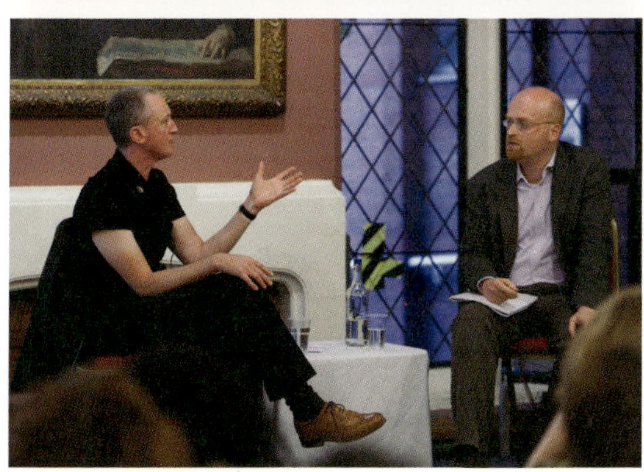

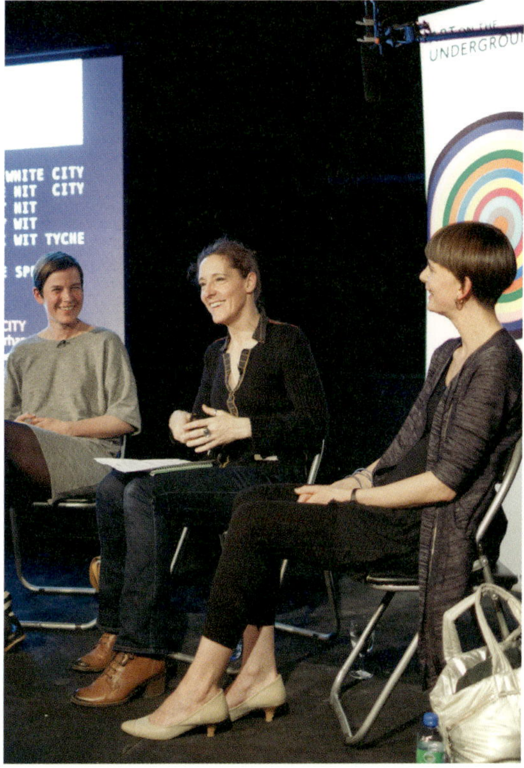

Clockwise from top left
Ruth Ewan speaking during the launch of *A LOCK IS A GATE*; Entrance to the premiere of *Who is Community?*; Bob and Roberta Smith and Tim Newton speaking during the launch of *Who is Community?*; Anna Barham, Alice Channer and Rachel Withers during the launches of *Hard Metal Body* and *WHITE CITY* and Michael Landy speaking during the launch of *Acts of Kindness*.

Acknowledgements

Artists
Art on the Underground would first and foremost like to thank the artists and writers for their dedication, vision and commitment in realising this ambitious and engaging series of projects in the ever-challenging context of London Underground.

Book
We are very grateful to Simon Elliott, Garry Blackburn, Rupert Gowar-Cliffe and Maja Hakenstad at Rose for their wonderful vision and dedication to this publication and each of the projects.

Thanks also to Federico Campagna and Mark Pagel for their original contributions to this publication, and to Kazys Varnelis for allowing us to reprint *The Meaning of Network Culture* in this context.

Projects
All our projects are realised due to the generosity and efforts of a great many people. We are grateful to our colleagues across London Underground for offering their time and expertise to this series, especially the Central line staff for their invaluable contributions, energy and generosity towards each project, and in particular those who participated in *Acts of Kindness*. Art on the Underground also wishes to thank Peter Tollington, General Manager of the Central line, for his unfailing support throughout this series.

Our appreciation also goes to all participants and collaborative organisations: Create Festival, Chisenhale Gallery, Whitechapel Gallery, Barbican Art Gallery, the Laburnum Boat Club, V&A Museum of Childhood, and all the Stratford Rising Organisations – including Stratford Circus, Stratford East Picture House, University of East London, Theatre Royal Stratford East, Rosetta Art Centre and The Nunnery.

We would also like to acknowledge everyone who contributed to the projects:

Acts of Kindness
François Chantala, Thomas Dane, London; Clive Lissaman; Scott Butcher, Anthony Farnan, Dave Johnson, Robert Peters and Gary Richardson, West Ruislip Depot, LU for their stories.

A LOCK IS A GATE
All the young people who took part; Cath Hawes, Dominic Hinshelwood, Rose Parnis, Tom Crawshaw, Peter Donaldson, Matt Dibble, Brian Farrow, David Leboff, Martin Tisdall, Lola Showunmi, Glenn Darlison, Laburnum Boat Club, Bethnal Green Tube station; Rebecca Branch, Josie Muirhead, A New Direction; Bridge Academy Music department; Peter Saunders, Lauriston Primary School.

Hard Metal Body
Jed Butterfield, Bob Pain, Omni; South London Gallery.

Who is Community?
Laura Capocefalo, Train Operations Standards Manager; George Foster, Duty Train Staff Manager; Simon Grove, Group Station Manager; Beth Hardisty, Stratford Circus; Donal Kelly, Train Operations Manager; Kirin Patel, Duty Service Manager; Dominic Voyce, Stratford East Picture House; Mark Winterflood, Train Operations Standards Manager.

Joana Borja, Cristian Cardenas, Flo Carter, Bradley Cumberbatch, Josh Darcy, Kara Dee, Glenn Doherty, Mike Fox, Stephen James, Mwape Nsofu, Teowa Pobjecky, Julia Rayner, John Kay Steel, Charlie Watkins.

Public Programmes
Rachael Williams, The Gate Theatre; Kendra du Toit, Toynbee Hall; Mark Vernon, Rachel Withers.

Photographers
Thierry Bal, Alastair Fyfe, Benedict Johnson, Daisy Hutchison.

Team
Rebecca Bell, Charlotte Bonham-Carter, Jiangee Ching, Claire Clutterbuck, Louise Coysh, Tamsin Dillon, Cathy Haynes, Snejana Krasteva, Josephine Martin, Lois Marshall, Jessica Molloy, Nick Triviais, Mariam Zulfiqar.

Funders
Jo Baxendale, Julie Lomax, Arts Council England.

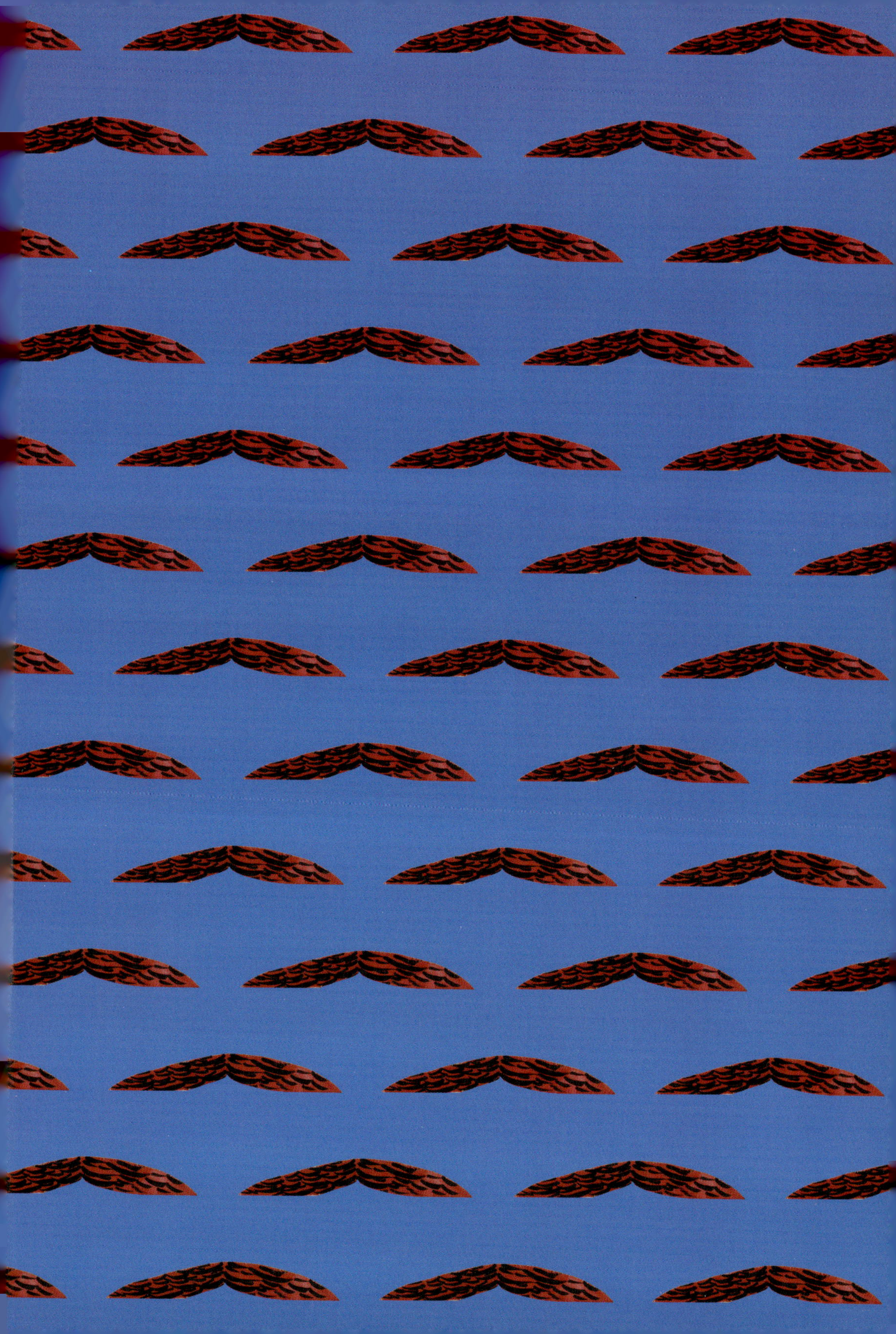

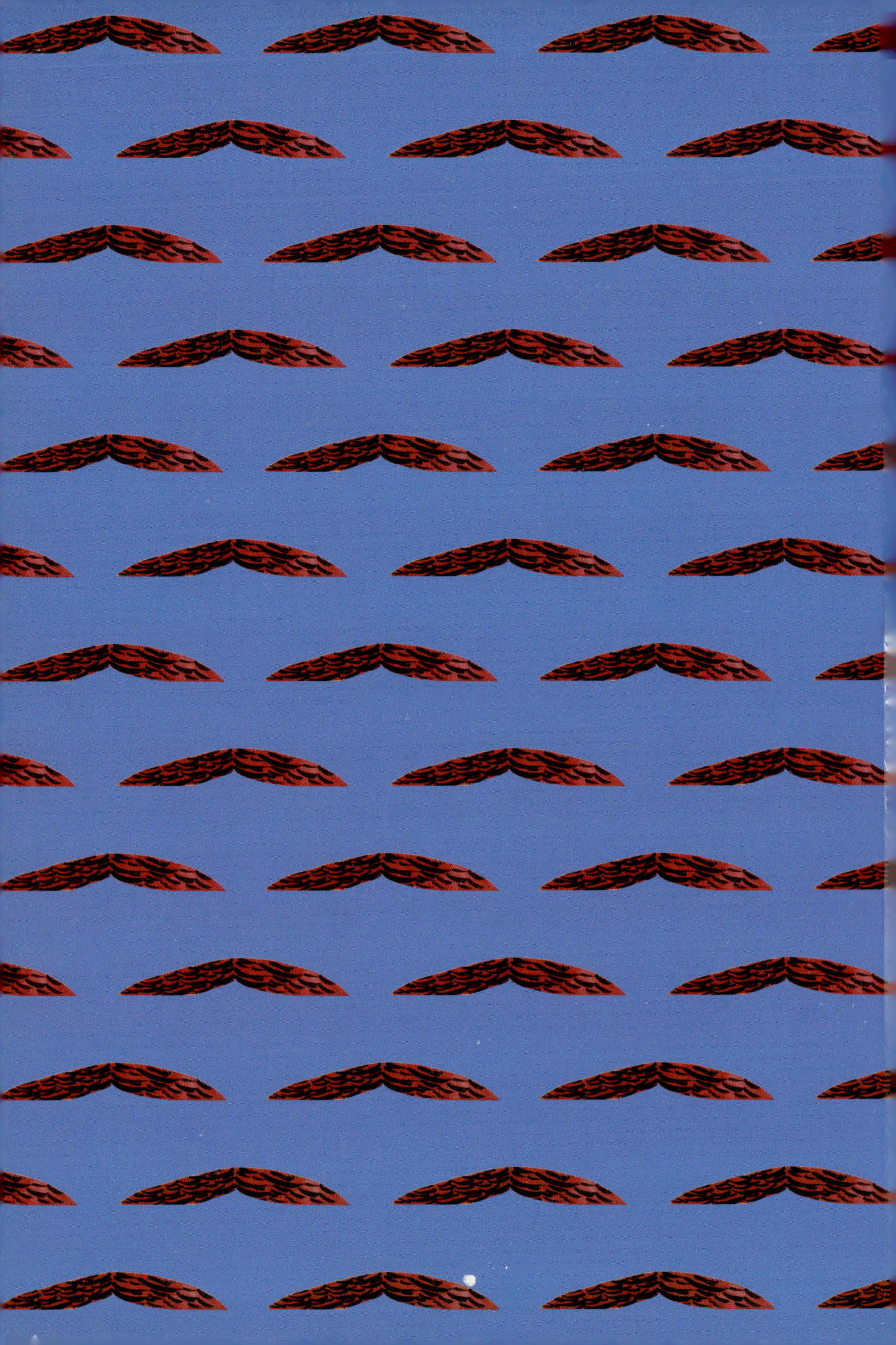